The Growth and Influence of Islam

IN THE NATIONS OF ASIA AND CENTRAL ASIA

Uzbekistan

The Growth and Influence of Islam
IN THE NATIONS OF ASIA AND CENTRAL ASIA

Afghanistan

Azerbaijan

Bangladesh

Indonesia

Islam in Asia: Facts and Figures

Islamism and Terrorist Groups in Asia

Kazakhstan

The Kurds

Kyrgyzstan

Malaysia

Muslims in China

Muslims in India

Muslims in Russia

Pakistan

Tajikistan

Turkmenistan

Uzbekistan

The Growth and Influence of Islam
IN THE NATIONS OF ASIA AND CENTRAL ASIA

Uzbekistan

Joyce Libal

Mason Crest Publishers
Philadelphia

Produced by OTTN Publishing, Stockton, New Jersey

Mason Crest Publishers
370 Reed Road
Broomall, PA 19008
www.masoncrest.com

First printing

1 3 5 7 9 8 6 4 2

Library of Congress Cataloging-in-Publication Data

Libal, Joyce.
  Uzbekistan / Joyce Libal.
    p. cm. -- (Growth and influence of Islam in the nations of Asia and
Central Asia)
  Includes bibliographical references and index.
  ISBN 1-59084-887-X
 1. Uzbekistan--Juvenile literature. I. Title. II. Series.
  DK948.66.L53 2005
  958.7--dc22
                              2004019823

The Growth and Influence of Islam
In the Nations of Asia and Central Asia

Table of Contents

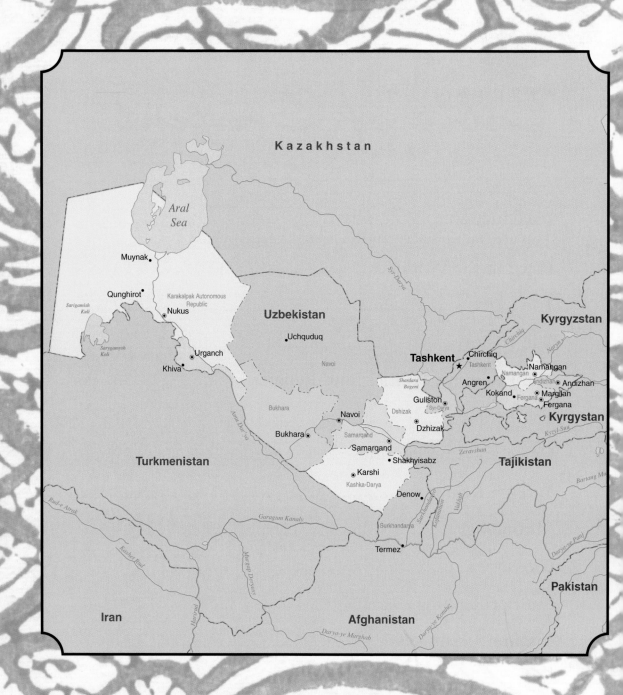

Governments include dictatorships, democracies, and hybrids without a name; centralized and decentralized administrations; and older patterns of tribal and clan associations. The region is a veritable encyclopedia of political expression.

Although such variety defies easy generalities, it is still possible to make several observations. First, the geopolitics of Central Asia and Asia reflect the impact of empires and the struggles of post-imperial independence. Central Asia, a historic corridor for traders and soldiers, was the scene of Russian expansion well into Soviet times. While Kazakhstan's leaders participated in the historic meeting of December 25, 1991, that dissolved the Soviet Union, the rest of the region's newly independent republics hardly expected it. They have found it difficult to grapple with a sometimes tenuous independence, buffeted by a strong residual Russian influence, the absence of settled institutions, the temptation of newly valuable natural resources, and mixed populations lacking a solid national identity. The shards of the Soviet Union have often been sharp—witness the Russian war in Chechnya—and sometimes fatal for those ambitious to grasp them.

Moving further east, one encounters an older devolution, that of the half-century since the British Raj dissolved into India and Pakistan (the latter giving violent birth to Bangladesh in 1971). Only recently, partly under the impact of the war on terrorism, have these nuclear-armed neighbors and adversaries found it possible to renew attempts at reconciliation. Still further east, Malaysia shares a British experience, but Indonesia has been influenced by its Dutch heritage. Even China defines its own borders along the lines of the Qing empire (the last pre-republican dynasty) at its most expansionist (including Tibet and Taiwan). These imperial histories lie heavily upon the politics of the region.

A second aspect worth noting is the variety of economic experimentation afoot in the area. State-dominated economic strategies, still in the ascendant, are separating government from the actual running of commerce and industry. "Privatization," however, is frequently a byword for crony capitalism and corruption. Yet in dynamic economies such as that of China, as well as an increasingly productive India, hundreds of millions of people have dramatically improved both their standard of living and their hope for the future. All of them aspire to benefit from international trade. Competitive advantages, such as low-cost labor (in some cases trained in high technology) and valuable natural resources (oil, gas, and minerals), promise much. This is indeed a revolution of rising expectations, some of which are being satisfied.

Yet more than corruption threatens this progress. Population increase, even though moderating, still overwhelms educational and employment opportunities. Many countries are marked by extremes of wealth and poverty, especially between rural and urban areas. Dangerous jealousies threaten ethnic groups (such as anti-Chinese violence in Indonesia). Hopelessly overburdened public services portend turmoil. Public health, never adequate, is harmed further by environmental damage to critical resources (such as the Aral Sea). By and large, Central Asian and Asian countries are living well beyond their infrastructures.

Third and finally, Islam has deeply affected the states and peoples of the region. Indonesia is the largest Muslim state in the world, and India hosts the second-largest Muslim population. Islam is not only the official religion of many states, it is the very reason for Pakistan's existence. But Islamic practices and groups vary: the well-known Sunni and Shiite groups are joined by energetic Salafi (Wahabi) and Sufi movements. Over the last 20 years especially, South and Central Asia have become battlegrounds for competing Shiite (Iranian) and Wahabi (Saudi) doctrines, well financed from abroad and aggressively antagonistic toward non-Muslims and each other. Resistance to the Soviet invasion of Afghanistan brought these groups battle-tested warriors and organizers. The war on terrorism has exposed just how far-reaching and active the new advocates of holy war (jihad) can be. Indonesia, in particular, is the scene of rivalry between

This newsstand in Tashkent offers many entertainment-oriented publications, but finding an independent newspaper or magazine in Uzbekistan is virtually impossible because of press censorship by the ruling Karimov regime.

an older, tolerant Islam and the jihadists. But Pakistan also faces an Islamic identity crisis. And India, wracked by sectarian strife, must hold together its democratic framework despite Muslim and Hindu extremists. This newly significant struggle within Islam, superimposed on an older Muslim history, will shape political and economic destinies throughout the region and beyond. Hence, the focus of our series.

We hope that these books will enlighten both teacher and student about a critical subject in a critical area of the world. Central Asia and Asia would be important in their own right to Americans; arguably, after 9/11, they became vital to our national security. And the enduring impact of Islam is a crucial factor we must understand. We at the Foreign Policy Research Institute hope these books will illuminate both the facts and the prospects.

Police investigators look for clues at the office of Uzbekistan's prosecutor general, one of several sites where terrorists detonated bombs in July 2004. Uzbekistan's secular government has blamed Islamists for a wave of recent deadly bombings.

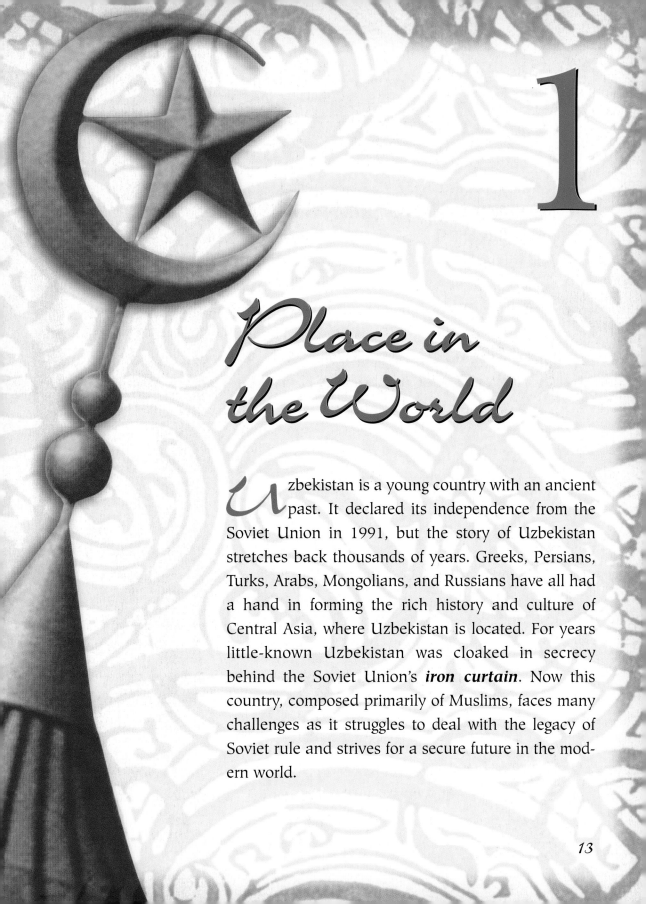

1

Place in the World

Uzbekistan is a young country with an ancient past. It declared its independence from the Soviet Union in 1991, but the story of Uzbekistan stretches back thousands of years. Greeks, Persians, Turks, Arabs, Mongolians, and Russians have all had a hand in forming the rich history and culture of Central Asia, where Uzbekistan is located. For years little-known Uzbekistan was cloaked in secrecy behind the Soviet Union's **iron curtain**. Now this country, composed primarily of Muslims, faces many challenges as it struggles to deal with the legacy of Soviet rule and strives for a secure future in the modern world.

Strategic Importance

Uzbekistan has the distinction of bordering all four of the other former Soviet republics of Central Asia (Kazakhstan, Kyrgyzstan, Tajikistan, and Turkmenistan). And Central Asia, in turn, is one of the world's most strategically important areas. To the north lies Russia; to the east, China. Along the southern border of Central Asia are Iran, Afghanistan (often considered part of Central Asia), and Pakistan, three nations that have figured prominently in the rise of militant, radical Islam and the global "war on terrorism."

Uzbekistan itself has been touched by Islamic extremism. In February 1999, a half-dozen car bombs killed 16 people and injured more than 150 in Tashkent, Uzbekistan's capital. In late March and early April 2004, five days of bomb blasts and gunfire again rocked Tashkent and communities near the city of Bukhara, claiming more than 45 lives. Two fundamentalist Muslim groups—the Islamic Movement of Uzbekistan and Hizb ut-Tahrir (Islamic Party of Liberation)—were blamed for the attacks. In July 2004, another wave of bombings occurred. These events drew an unusual level of international attention to a country that is typically overlooked.

The Islamic Movement of Uzbekistan (IMU) is an extremist faction believed to have links with al-Qaeda, the international network of Islamic fundamentalist terrorists led by Saudi dissident Osama bin Laden. IMU members fought side by side with al-Qaeda and the Taliban (Afghanistan's Islamist regime) during the 2001 U.S.-led war in Afghanistan, which was launched in response to the September 11 terrorist attacks on New York City and Washington, D.C. Hizb ut-Tahrir is often suspected of helping organize terrorist attacks, although this 50-year-old organization claims to use nonviolent means to reach its goals.

U.S. policymakers consider Uzbekistan important to American security interests. Since 2001 the United States has operated a major military installation, the Karshi-Khanabad Air Base, from Uzbekistan's Kashka-

Darya Province. The base served as a launching pad for operations in Afghanistan, with which Uzbekistan shares a border, and it continues to be a significant asset in regional operations in the "war on terror." More fundamentally, the United States is deeply interested in preventing Islamic extremism from taking root among Uzbekistan's 26 million residents—who constitute half of the total population of the former Soviet republics of Central Asia—and has emphasized the need for the development of **secular** democracy and economic stability as a safeguard against that outcome. Yet political and economic reforms have been slow in coming.

Challenges of Independence

About the same size as California, Uzbekistan was the fourth-largest republic in the Soviet Union, and today it is the most densely inhabited country in Central Asia. Its location, large population, and rich natural resources (primarily gold, natural gas, and oil) are all factors that could help Uzbekistan emerge as a prosperous country. But progress has been impeded by powerful regional clans, which place self-interest above national interest; their opposition to anything that threatens their control has had the effect of preserving the status quo. Also, ethnic tensions linger, due in no small measure to the arbitrary nature of the Soviet Union's republic divisions established during the 1920s under Soviet dictator Joseph Stalin.

Uzbekistanis have faced a series of formidable obstacles in recent years. These include a disappointing economy, environmental degradation, and political and ethnic unrest. In addition, the country is confronting a demographic time bomb: 60 percent of the population is under 25, and unless jobs can be created for this large group, massive instability may ensue.

Uzbekistan is already one of the world's major producers of natural gas. The construction of additional pipelines could make Central Asia's natural gas and oil available to the world market and thus bring prosperity to

Uzbekistan. But this development has been hindered by border disputes, unrest caused by Islamic militants, problems with Uzbekistan's currency, and a series of government decisions that have left foreign investors wary.

Despite the great potential of Uzbekistan's natural gas reserves, the national economy has largely been locked into cotton production. Overdependence on this crop has had devastating environmental consequences, most visibly in the shrinking of the country's largest body of water, the Aral Sea. According to scientists, so much water is being diverted for irrigation from the rivers that feed the sea that by 2020 the Aral—once the world's fourth-largest inland body of water—may no longer exist. **Desertification** caused by shrinkage of the sea, which has lost more than half of its surface area since 1960, is a major ecological threat and has caused serious health problems for much of the country's population. Costs associated with these health problems put a strain on Uzbekistan's economy.

In the political sphere, while Uzbekistan claims to be a republic, in reality its government rules in an **authoritarian** manner. Almost a decade and a half since gaining independence, the country has yet to hold free and open presidential elections. The arrest and imprisonment of **political dissidents** and those who practice Islam outside of government-sanctioned mosques is widespread—as many as 5,800 of these Muslims were being incarcerated as of late 2004, according to the U.S. Department of State. In addition, Uzbekistani authorities routinely use torture against government critics and suspects, according to the State Department, Human Rights Watch, Amnesty International, and other independent human-rights advocacy groups.

Nongovernmental organizations (NGOs)—private groups dedicated to social service, humanitarian assistance, environmental protection, economic development, and the like—face substantial political barriers in Uzbekistan. In May 2004 the government forced the Open Society Institute (OSI), one of the world's largest and most respected international NGOs, to

A young man sits atop an abandoned fishing boat near the village of Muynak, which was once a port on the Aral Sea. As the sea has receded, Muynak and other former fishing villages in Uzbekistan have found themselves miles from the water.

close its foundation in Uzbekistan. That same year, the European Bank for Reconstruction and Development (EBRD) announced that because of a lack of positive reforms in Uzbekistan, it would reduce its activities in the country. In July 2004 the United States "de-certified" Uzbekistan for its human rights violations.

Still, advocates urge Western countries to have patience with the slow—even indiscernible—pace of reform in Uzbekistan. They argue that continued engagement with this Muslim country is vital to the overall effort to combat Islamic extremism. And, as various experts point out, authoritarian regimes have been the rule, rather than the exception, in countries going through a transition from communism to a democratic, free market system. Whether or not Uzbekistan does progress on the path toward social and economic reform remains to be seen. However, its strategic importance—to the United States as well as to other world powers—is likely to increase in the coming decades.

A small community nestled near a lake in the Chatkal Mountains, which form the northern boundary of Uzbekistan.

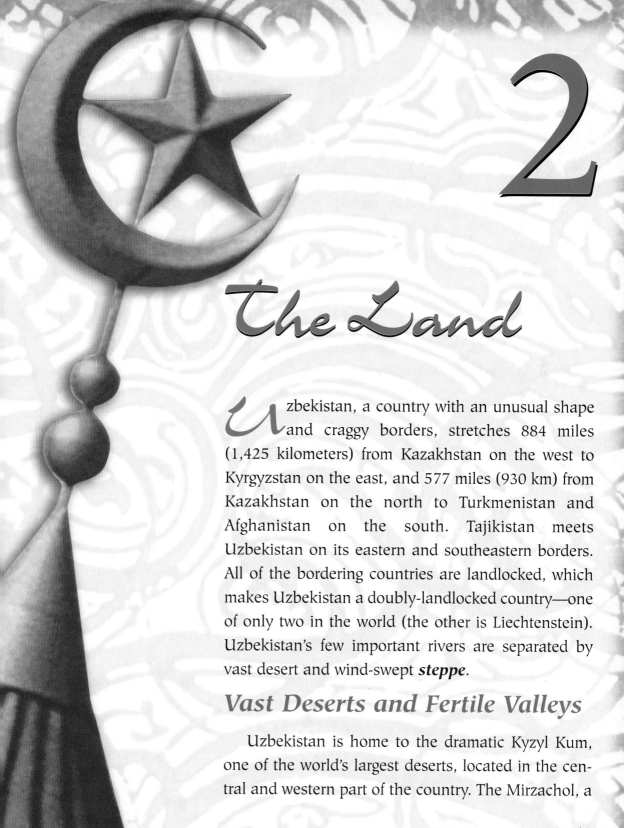

2

The Land

Uzbekistan, a country with an unusual shape and craggy borders, stretches 884 miles (1,425 kilometers) from Kazakhstan on the west to Kyrgyzstan on the east, and 577 miles (930 km) from Kazakhstan on the north to Turkmenistan and Afghanistan on the south. Tajikistan meets Uzbekistan on its eastern and southeastern borders. All of the bordering countries are landlocked, which makes Uzbekistan a doubly-landlocked country—one of only two in the world (the other is Liechtenstein). Uzbekistan's few important rivers are separated by vast desert and wind-swept *steppe*.

Vast Deserts and Fertile Valleys

Uzbekistan is home to the dramatic Kyzyl Kum, one of the world's largest deserts, located in the central and western part of the country. The Mirzachol, a desert that is much smaller than the Kyzyl Kum, lies to the southwest of Tashkent in northeastern Uzbekistan. The vast Ustyurt Plateau, which forms the far western part of the country, contains desert, streams, marshes, and some low mountain ridges.

Much of the land of Uzbekistan is inhospitable. Throughout the centuries human settlement clustered around the fertile river valleys and oases in the eastern regions of the modern-day country. Although extinct today, Caspian tigers once roamed the forested parts of these river valleys. The word used in Uzbekistan for these forests is *tugai*, named after the dense brush native to the forests. Grassy areas and wetlands are also located in the river valleys and form extremely important wildlife habitats.

Rivers that were once wild are today harnessed and controlled by countless dams and canals. These structures were built to increase the amount of **arable** land through extensive irrigation. But massive and poorly managed irrigation projects from Soviet times have resulted in the overuse of water and the depletion of the soil. As irrigated water percolates down through the ground in many areas, salt is dissolved and forced to the surface, resulting in increased soil salinity.

The remaining farmland that is fertile is located in river valleys and on plains near mountains. The most fertile area of the country is the Fergana Valley. This region, which is more than 180 miles (290 km) long, cuts into Kyrgyzstan and Tajikistan and forms Uzbekistan's easternmost edge.

Mountains and Lakes

More than two-thirds of Uzbekistan is flat, but rugged mountain ranges in Kazakhstan, Kyrgyzstan, and Tajikistan creep into the country along its northeastern, eastern, and southeastern borders. These ranges receive more rain and snow than the rest of Uzbekistan. This precipitation collects in the mountains, and the water then flows into the country's critically important rivers. The foothills of the Pamirs, a dramatic mountain range

A river flows through the foothills of the Pamir Mountains, near the border with Afghanistan. This region in southeastern Uzbekistan contains the country's highest peak, Adelunga Toghi.

covering Tajikistan and Kyrgyzstan, are found in southeastern Uzbekistan. These hills are the site of the country's highest elevation, Adelunga Toghi, which rises 14,107 feet (4,301 meters) above sea level.

Lake Aydarkul, located in the northeast, is the largest natural freshwater lake in Uzbekistan. There are also several artificial lakes and reservoirs in the country. In the northwestern region Uzbekistan and Kazakhstan share the Aral Sea.

Earthquakes can occur in many parts of the country, particularly in the mountain areas. Significant earthquakes were recorded in the Fergana Valley in 1823, 1889, 1902, and 1926. Destructive quakes took place in Tashkent in 1866, 1868, and 1966.

The Geography of Uzbekistan

Location: Central Asia, north of Afghanistan
Area: slightly larger than California
    total: 174,486 square miles (447,400 sq km)
    land: 165,906 square miles (425,400 sq km)
    water: 8,580 square miles (22,000 sq km)
Borders: Afghanistan, 85 miles (137 km); Kazakhstan,
    1,366 miles (2,203 km); Kyrgyzstan, 681 miles (1,099
    km); Tajikistan, 720 miles (1,161 km); Turkmenistan,
    1,005 miles (1,621 km)
Climate: mostly midlatitude desert, with long, hot summers
    and mild winters; semiarid in eastern grasslands
Terrain: mostly flat-to-rolling sandy desert with dunes;
    broad, flat, intensely irrigated river valleys along
    course of Amu Dar'ya, Syr Dar'ya, and Zarafshon;
    Fergana Valley in east surrounded by mountainous
    Tajikistan and Kyrgyzstan; shrinking Aral Sea in west
Elevation extremes:
    lowest point: Sariqarnish Kuli, 39 feet (12 meters) below
      sea level
    highest point: Adelunga Toghi, 14,107 feet (4,301
      meters)
Natural hazards: occasional earthquakes

Source: Adapted from CIA World Factbook, 2004.

Climate

Uzbekistan experiences four seasons. In general, summers are hot and winters are cool. However, temperatures can vary widely within a single day, and at various altitudes. In some desert areas, daily temperatures fluctuate by as much as 68° Fahrenheit (20° Celsius). Temperatures in the summer often hover around 90°F (32°C), but they can reach 104°F

(40°C)—and sometimes climb as high as 122°F (50°C) in certain desert areas. During the comparatively mild winters, average temperatures range between 23°F and 50°F (–5°C and 10°C), though extremely cold temperatures may occur on occasion.

With the exception of the higher altitudes in the mountains, little rain falls in this arid land. The dry climate is largely the product of Uzbekistan's distance from oceans and the mountains along its borders, which block water vapor from reaching the country's interior and falling as rain. The vast majority of Uzbekistan receives only 4 to 8 inches (10 to 20 centimeters) of rain annually, but parts of the Kyzyl Kum may get less than 0.5 inch (1.25 cm). Even in the fertile Fergana Valley, yearly precipitation rarely exceeds 12 inches (30 cm). Most of the rain arrives in spring (March through April) and late fall (October through November). Winters are comparatively wet around Tashkent and the Fergana Valley; while winter precipitation may fall in the form of snow, it usually melts quickly. With the exception of the dry summer months of July and August, the weather in the mountains is unpredictable throughout the year. The heavy snows that fall in these altitudes can make travel through mountain passes hazardous.

During the hottest time of the year, mountain glaciers begin to melt, adding to the water flow of Uzbekistan's rivers. Some change in climate has resulted from the dramatic reduction in the water volume of the Aral Sea; since 1950, Uzbekistan has experienced an increasing number of rainless days.

The Fergana Valley

Most of the lush Fergana Valley lies within Uzbekistan. More than 6 million people live in this valley, which occupies approximately 8,500 square miles (22,000 sq km) and is hugged by a series of mountain ridges. Sometimes called the Pearl of Central Asia, this broad, flat, and heavily irrigated area has been an important agricultural center since ancient times. Today, it is both the most fertile and the most densely populated land in the region, which makes it vital to Uzbekistan's economy.

The Kuramin mountain range, located southeast of Tashkent and extending into Tajikistan, forms the Fergana's northwestern border. The main feature of the range, the Kamchik Pass, is divided by a two-lane highway that is edged with snowcapped mountains and provides a dramatic entrance into the beautiful Fergana Valley. Located approximately 40 miles (70 km) east of Tashkent are the Chatkal Mountains, which extend into Kyrgyzstan and form the valley's northern boundary. The Turkestan range, which is part of the Pamirs, lies south of the city of Fergana.

A farmer walks through a cotton field in the Fergana Valley. This lush region contains some of the most fertile farmland in Central Asia.

Much of the silk, grain, and cotton production of Uzbekistan takes place in the Fergana Valley. Orchards and vineyards are abundant, as are walnut groves. Natural gas, oil, and iron ore are also mined in the region.

The Kyzyl Kum

Dominating the west, north, and central parts of the country is the vast Kyzyl Kum, whose red color comes from minerals in the soil. Kyzyl Kum (or Qyzylqum in the Turkic language) means "Red Sand." Most of the approximately 115,000 square miles (300,000 sq km) of land making up this desert is flat and slopes toward the northwest. In some areas, barren, isolated mountains rise from the desert floor. In the central and southwestern regions of the desert, strong winds push the sand into ridges and dunes that can stand as tall as 300 feet (90 meters).

Many desert plants bloom for short periods during April in the Kyzyl Kum. One prominent animal living in the region is the grey monitor lizard, which can grow as long as 5 feet (1.6 meters). Several varieties of rodents and the Central Asian turtle also live in the desert, as do many birds.

In the past, little attention was given to preserving the habitat of the Kyzyl Kum, though in recent years the government and concerned wildlife groups have focused on the region's needs. They are just as concerned with rural development as they are with preservation, and attempts have been made to integrate these goals. Leading this coordinated effort is the Nuratau-Kyzylkum Biosphere Reserve Project, which works under the direction of the State Committee for Nature Protection and receives some funding from the United Nations Development Programme.

Three Great Rivers

Only about 12 percent of Uzbekistan's land area is used for growing crops, and much of that land is irrigated. Not surprisingly, more than 60 percent of the population lives where the farmland is richest—along rivers and in irrigated areas.

The broad Amu Dar'ya (*dar'ya* means "river") begins in the Pamir Mountains. It flows in a westward direction along the border of Afghanistan and then in a northwesterly direction through Turkmenistan, parallel with the Uzbekistan border, before turning at Khiva and heading north through Uzbekistan toward the Aral Sea. For hundreds of miles, the current is swift. However, by the time it reaches the Kara-Kum (Black Sands), a desert in Turkmenistan, the current slows considerably. There the river stands as a natural border between the Kara-Kum and the Kyzyl Kum.

Called the Oxus in ancient times, the Amu Dar'ya forms an important fertile valley and finally a **delta** where rich soil is deposited. The river once

The broad Amu Dar'ya, pictured here near Khiva, is one of Uzbekistan's major rivers.

replenished the Aral Sea where it entered at the southern end, though today excessive irrigation along the length of the river depletes the water long before it reaches that point.

Much of the forest that once stood along the shores of the Amu Dar'ya has been destroyed, the trees cleared away to convert the land into cotton farms. Several nature reserves have been established in an effort to protect the remaining forest habitat.

The Zeravshan River begins in the mountains of Tajikistan and flows into the center of Uzbekistan from east to west. The Zeravshan River valley constitutes one of the most important oases in Central Asia. After passing Samarqand (also spelled Samarkand) and Bukhara, the river dries up in the Kyzyl Kum. It was a longer river 30 years ago, but much water has since been diverted for agricultural purposes. This area is home to several bird species, including the night heron, white-winged woodpecker, and several warblers, as well as types of buntings, finches, and nuthatches. Bukhara deer, which were once plentiful in Uzbekistan's tugai, are being reintroduced to the region in the Zeravshan Nature Reserve.

The Syr Dar'ya is a major river that Uzbekistan shares with Tajikistan, Kyrgyzstan, and Kazakhstan. Called the Jaxartes in ancient times, the river originates in the Alai Mountains in the Fergana Valley, at the junction of the Naryn Dar'ya and Kara Dar'ya. The Syr Dar'ya forms the northern border of the Kyzyl Kum and then empties into the northeastern part of the Aral Sea. The Syr Dar'ya is a great source of water, though because it is shallow it is not very important for navigation. As with other shared rivers, water use and quality are points of contention among the Central Asian republics.

Several smaller rivers also run through Uzbekistan. Like the major rivers, these rivers suffer from a variety of serious pollution problems. Sources of contamination include agricultural processing plants, chemical plants, and wastewater treatment facilities. Excessive use of pesticides and fertilizers has also contributed significantly to the degradation of the water.

A Shrinking Sea

The Aral Sea is now among the world's most significant man-made disasters. Its water reserve, which depends on the inflow of the Syr Dar'ya and Amu Dar'ya, first began to drop in the 1960s when the Soviet Union increased irrigation by millions of acres to boost the cotton crop. With water evaporating from the sea every day and reduced amounts of new water to replenish the volume, the sea began to shrink. Today, the area occupied by this sea is only half as large as it once was. Because the sea's surface area has been reduced, less water evaporates and, consequently, less precipitation falls on nearby areas. Decreased surface area has also resulted in greater climate extremes, making the summers hotter and the winters colder.

The Aral once supported a profitable fishing industry, but pollution and the sea's increased salt content (caused by the loss of water) have decimated the fish population. Additionally, large salt flats now occupy approximately 15,500 square miles (39,744 sq km) that were once covered by water, creating a desolate wasteland. Some people have even started calling this area the Aral Desert. Pollutants that once found their way into Uzbekistan's rivers now lie on this exposed seabed. Wind blows the polluted sand great distances, causing eye and skin irritation, respiratory illnesses, and even, it is believed, certain cancers for people in affected areas.

Most scientists do not think the Aral Sea can be restored to its past glory, but they hope to save what remains and stop the downward spiral of pollution that the ecosystem is facing. They also want to save the existing river deltas from further destruction. To accomplish this, the scientists believe, it will be necessary to stop any additional water usage, convert

This NASA satellite image shows the Aral Sea, which straddles the border between Kazakhstan and northern Uzbekistan. The Aral was once the world's fourth-largest inland sea, but irrigation projects caused it to shrink so much that by the late 1980s it had separated into two bodies of water, as shown here. Despite regional efforts to stop or reverse this ecological disaster, the sea continues to lose about 23 square miles (60 sq km) of surface area a year.

more cultivated land to crops other than cotton and rice (which require huge amounts of water), and step up other conservation measures.

Plants and Animals

The diverse topography and habitats of Uzbekistan support a variety of wildlife, but widespread irrigation, use of land for agriculture, and environmental degradation pose threats to many species. One such species is the saiga antelope, which shares Uzbekistan's steppes with an assortment of more abundant mammals, including foxes, wolves, badgers, and deer. Hawks, falcons, partridge, and grouse also inhabit the steppes, parts of which are covered with low shrubs and drought-resistant native grasses.

Mammals living in forested river valleys include the wild boar, tolai hare, jackal, onager (a type of Asiatic ass), and dormouse. Bats and birds, including owls, pheasants, and kestrels, are also found here. Several threatened and endangered bird species migrate along Uzbekistan's forested waterways. Some species from parts of Siberia and Kazakhstan winter in this habitat, which features poplar, willow, and elm trees, as well as smaller shrubby plants such as honeysuckle.

Bukhara deer are among the rarer animals in the tugai. Otters are also rare and appear only occasionally in the open. Goitered gazelles come into the tugai from the surrounding desert; only 300 to 400 of these once widely ranging Asian antelopes are believed to remain in the world. A conservation project is under way in the province of Surkhandarya, located at the country's southern tip and bordering Afghanistan and Tajikistan. The project's focus is on the study of certain rare species, including a type of wild goat known as the markhor.

Uzbekistan's remote eastern mountains are home to the endangered snow leopard, a big cat that, though officially protected, is hunted illegally for its beautiful fur. Boar, brown bear, lynx, and various types of wild goats are among the more common animals found in highland areas. Among the most interesting species is the alpine ibex, a kind of mountain goat that has long, backward-curving horns. The mountains are also home to eagles, vultures, and other birds. Trees that grow at higher elevations include larch and evergreens such as juniper and spruce.

Cattails and reeds grow near the shores of water reservoirs, providing a suitable habitat for countless bird varieties. Common species that nest in these areas include the great cormorant, grey heron, and little egret; rarer inhabitants include the Dalmation pelican and white-headed duck.

Many bird species migrate through Uzbekistan. The Ustyurt Plateau's marshes, in the far western part of the country, are along a particularly important *flyway.*

Reptiles and amphibians are also found in Uzbekistan. Caspian and swamp turtles, various geckos, skinks (small lizards), and the Central Asian cobra are just a few of the species that live in the country.

This ancient Zoroastrian fire temple still stands in Bukhara; the flame is fueled by natural gas seeping through the ground. Zoroastrianism, which originated in Persia, was an important religion in the Uzbekistan region before the arrival of Islam.

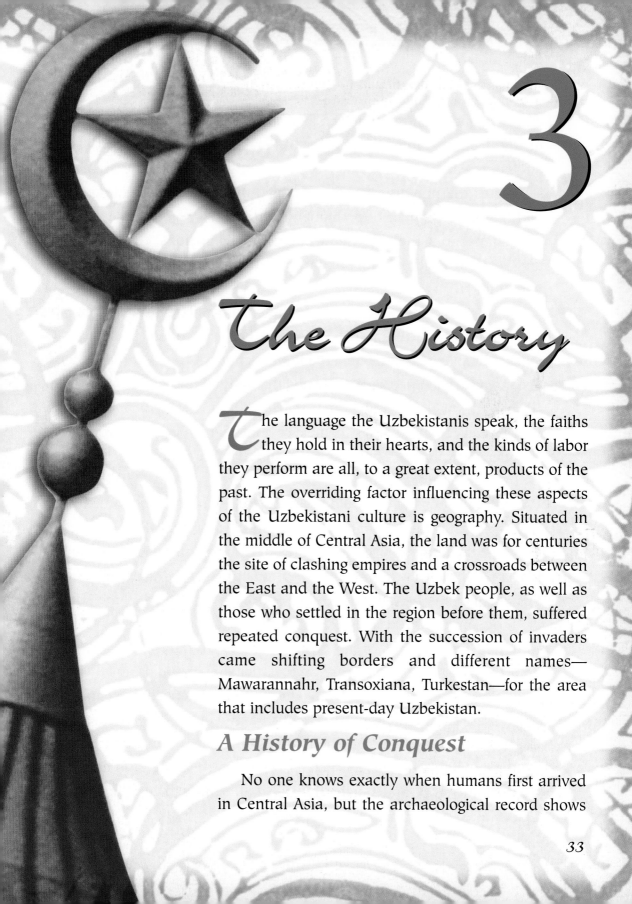

3

The History

The language the Uzbekistanis speak, the faiths they hold in their hearts, and the kinds of labor they perform are all, to a great extent, products of the past. The overriding factor influencing these aspects of the Uzbekistani culture is geography. Situated in the middle of Central Asia, the land was for centuries the site of clashing empires and a crossroads between the East and the West. The Uzbek people, as well as those who settled in the region before them, suffered repeated conquest. With the succession of invaders came shifting borders and different names—Mawarannahr, Transoxiana, Turkestan—for the area that includes present-day Uzbekistan.

A History of Conquest

No one knows exactly when humans first arrived in Central Asia, but the archaeological record shows clear evidence of human presence in the area of today's Uzbekistan during the Ice Age. **Nomadic** peoples of Persian origin are believed to have arrived as early as 1000 B.C. The use of irrigation, with the area's rivers serving as the primary resource, enabled the development of agriculture and the establishment of permanent settlements. Some of the cities that took shape along the rivers grew into great civilizations, centers for trade, and seats of government. Bukhara, Khiva, and Samarqand all became important **city-states**.

In the sixth century B.C., the Persian Achaemenid dynasty brought much of Central Asia, including present-day Uzbekistan, under its control. The Persian Empire held sway until the fourth century B.C. In 331 Alexander the Great of Macedon decisively defeated the army of the Persian king, Darius III, at Gaugamela in present-day Iraq. By the following year the Persian Empire had collapsed. Over the next several years, Alexander proceeded to conquer Central Asia, bringing Greek culture to the region.

In the centuries after Alexander the Great, a mix of Eastern and Western religious beliefs could be found in Central Asia, testament to the region's location at an important cultural crossroads. For hundreds of years the dominant religion in the area of Uzbekistan was Zoroastrianism. One of the world's oldest faiths, Zoroastrianism—which originated in Persia sometime between 2000 and 600 B.C.—teaches that the supreme God, or Ahura Mazda, is locked in a cosmic struggle with the evil spirit Ahriman. Believers, who expect the ultimate triumph of Ahura Mazda, help the poor, offer sacrifices, and participate in rituals involving fire. Buddhism is another Eastern religion that was practiced in Central Asia. Originating in India around the fifth century B.C., it was spread into Central Asia largely along trade routes. Judaism, Christianity, and an extinct religion known as Manichaeism (which originated in Persia in the third century A.D. and taught that all matter is evil) also flourished in Central Asia before the seventh century.

The Silk Road—which was actually a network of trade routes rather than a single way—connected China with the Mediterranean world via Central Asia. Its origins, as well as its name, stem from Roman demand for the exquisite fabric that in ancient times only the Chinese knew how to make. But over the centuries, camel caravans carried a variety of goods between East and West across the vast Asian landscape. The trade brought wealth, power, and cultural diversity to Central Asia, and major cities along the way—including Bukhara, Khiva, Samarqand, and Tashkent—became centers for art, science, and religion.

The Coming of Islam and Arab Rule

The popularity of all other religions practiced in Central Asia would be eclipsed by a new faith first brought to the region in the mid-seventh century: Islam. The central human figure in Islam is the prophet Muhammad, who was born in Mecca (present-day Saudi Arabia) around A.D. 570. Muslims, as adherents of Islam are called, believe that Muhammad began receiving revelations from Allah (the Arabic word for God) around 610; the revelations were later written down in the Qur'an (or Koran), the holy book of Islam. Muhammad began preaching Allah's message—the essence of which is that there is only one God and that people must submit to God's will—but opposition among the idol-worshiping, **polytheistic** Meccans was fierce, and the Muslims were forced to flee Mecca in 622. After a period of warfare, however, they returned triumphantly to Mecca in 630.

After the Prophet's death in 632, his followers began spreading the new religion beyond the Arabian Peninsula. Arab armies first invaded Central Asia in the mid-seventh century, and by 750 the Arab Abbasid **caliphate** was in control of the region and Islam was firmly established there. The

This mausoleum in Bukhara was built around A.D. 907 as a tomb for the Samanid ruler Ismail I. The Samanid dynasty (819–999) was the first native ruling dynasty to emerge in the Transoxiana region of Central Asia after the Muslim Arab conquest.

Arabs introduced a written alphabet, and Arabic replaced Persian as the language used for trade and government (intellectuals continued to use Persian, however). The region prospered under the Arabs, and important cities along the Silk Road—the main trading route between Europe and Asia—maintained their status as centers of trade and culture.

Eventually, however, Abbasid power declined, and various Persian groups began to regain control of Central Asia from the Arabs. Persian was reinstated as the official language, and in 819 the Samanids became the first *indigenous* rulers in the wake of the Arab conquest. The Samanid dynasty—which would endure until 999—initiated an economic and intellectual revival and transformed Bukhara into a center of learning. But in the end it was unable to withstand pressures from another ethnic group: the Turks.

The Turks

From the ninth century on, Samanid rulers had forced Turks—traditionally nomadic tribesmen from the vast steppes of Asia—to serve in their armies. Eventually, several ambitious Turk soldiers saw and seized opportunities to carve out some territory for themselves at the expense of the Samanids. These victories, in turn, attracted other Turkic tribes to the area, spelling the end of Samanid rule.

At the beginning of the 11th century, another group of Turks, led by the Seljuks, conquered the territory then known as Khwarazm (or Khorezm). This region included land both north and south of the Amu Dar'ya. The Seljuks eventually ruled a huge territory that was later split between several Persian and Turkic rulers. In the 12th century, Khwarazm (in present-day western Uzbekistan) and Iran were united. During all these political shifts, the area continued to prosper and the local culture remained generally untouched, a situation that was due in large measure to the tolerance espoused by the various rulers. All that would change, however, with the arrival of yet another invading force.

Genghis Khan and the Rule of Timur

In the early part of the 13th century, a huge army led by the Mongol conqueror Genghis Khan (also spelled Jenghiz Khan) swept through Central Asia. The region of Khwarazm and cities such as Bukhara suffered greatly at the hands of the fearsome warriors from the east, who massacred tens of thousands of people and wreaked widespread destruction, pillaging conquered towns and cities and damaging irrigation networks. Although Genghis's army came to be known as the Mongol horde, many of its soldiers were actually of Turkic, rather than Mongol, origin. As these conquering soldiers settled in the Uzbekistan region—and as other Turkic nomads migrated to the area—Turkic people came to constitute a majority of the region's population.

After Genghis Khan died in 1227, the empire he had amassed was divided among his sons and grandsons, who each took on the title of khan, or leader. Genghis's son Chagatai inherited the **khanate** of Central Asia, which included the region of Uzbekistan.

The empire began to break up in the 14th century as tribal leaders

Timur Lenk (inset) was one of history's most ruthless conquerors. As a young man Timur (1336–1405) set out to reconstitute the vast Mongol empire of Genghis Khan, which had become divided after Genghis's death. Timur's armies plundered cities from Persia to Russia and throughout Central Asia. Notorious for his brutality—Timur often made piles of his victims' skulls as memorials to his victories—he was also a patron of the arts and sought to make Samarqand, his capital, the greatest city in the world. His architects constructed numerous exquisite buildings and monuments— among them the mausoleum complex at Shah-i Zinda (pictured here), where several of Timur's relatives are buried.

competed with one another. One of those leaders was Timur Lenk (known also as Tamerlane), a fearless warrior who today remains a revered figure in Uzbekistani history. Timur first won control over the tribes in Transoxiana—the region covering modern-day Uzbekistan and south-western Kazakhstan. He went on to conquer a very large territory that encompassed western Central Asia; land north of the Aral Sea; some areas between the Black Sea and the Mediterranean; and the lands of present-day Iran, Iraq, and India. He established the empire's capital at Samarqand, a city not far from his birthplace. Although millions of people died in his conquests, Timur also supported scientific research, brought scholars and artists to the capital, and commissioned the construction of many impressive buildings. While attempting to invade China in 1405, he died of an illness. Following his death, the empire was marred by internal conflict for nearly a century.

Uzbek Rule

At the beginning of the 16th century, nomadic tribes from the area north of the Aral Sea, under the leadership of Shaybani Khan, invaded the land now known as Uzbekistan. These people, who were of Turkic origin, called themselves Uzbeks, a name that some historians believe was taken from a former leader.

By 1510 the Uzbeks had conquered Central Asia. They established three khanates, or primary bases of political control: Bukhara, Khiva (which was basically the former area of Khwarazm), and Kokand (in the Fergana Valley). Of these, the Bukhara Khanate, led by the Shaybanids, was the most powerful. Until 1750, for example, much of the area that is now Afghanistan was under the control of Bukhara.

During the reign of the Shaybanids, which reached its apex in the late 16th century, trade along the Silk Road greatly declined as the discoveries of European explorers opened up ocean routes between Europe and China and India. Looking for more trade opportunities, the Shaybanids expanded their trade with Russia during the 16th and 17th centuries.

The Shaybanid reign ended in the early 17th century and was replaced by the Janid dynasty. During the 17th and 18th centuries, Kazakhs and Turkmen launched several attacks on the Uzbek khanates. In an effort to defeat the invaders, the khan who controlled Khiva asked for aid from the Russian czar Peter the Great. The czar granted the request by sending an army in 1717, but for reasons that historians can only speculate about today, the khan attacked and routed the Russians as they entered Khiva.

The Coming of the Russians

Russia's interest in Central Asia developed concurrently with England's growing involvement during the 19th century. Czar Nicholas I wanted to prevent England from gaining a foothold in the region. Interestingly, the Civil War in the United States (1861–1865) also played a part in Russia's strategy. When the war interrupted the exportation of U.S. cotton, Russian leaders decided to establish a more secure source of the fiber elsewhere. By that point, Central Asia was already producing cotton.

Between 1865 and 1873, Russia conquered the areas of Karakalpakstan, Bukhara, Samarqand, Tashkent, and Khiva. In 1867 Tashkent became the capital of the newly named region of Russian Turkestan, which by 1876 included lands of all the present-day Central Asian republics. However, with the exception of Tashkent and the khanate of Kokand, which Russian governors controlled, the khans of Uzbekistan were allowed to maintain authority over their lands.

All foreign trade in the territory fell to Russian authorities, who immediately began to increase cotton production. The new emphasis on cotton farming had a negative impact on many peasant farmers because their limited acreage precluded them from also growing all the vegetables and other crops they needed.

In the 1890s Russia connected railroads to Russian Turkestan. These new transportation links carried increasing numbers of Russian immigrants to the region, which had affordable land and a comparatively appealing climate. Most of the newcomers settled in populated areas. Soon ethnic unrest began to develop between native Uzbeks and the Russian population.

By the end of the 19th century, the khanates of Khiva and Bukhara retained little actual power, as the Turkestan governor-general, who answered to Czar Nicholas II, exerted real authority over the region. This helped fuel growing unrest among the Uzbek population, and several revolts against czarist Russia—often led by religious leaders— erupted during this time. In response, Russia tightened its control in the khanates.

In the face of Russian domination, many Uzbeks, like other Turkic peoples of Central Asia, turned to a movement called Jadidism. The Jadidists sought to preserve their Islamic and Turkic culture, but they also promoted secular education and other reform efforts designed to modernize their societies. The movement's leaders were young intellectuals, many of whose families were members of the wealthy merchant class. Some had attended Muslim schools locally and then gone on to Russian universities; others had studied in Istanbul, Turkey. By the beginning of the 20th century, as the Jadidists began promoting independence, Uzbek khans appeased their Russian superiors by repressing the movement. Many Jadidists were forced into exile as Russia and the Bukhara and Khiva khanates cracked down on political dissidents.

The Soviet Era

Until World War I, Central Asians under Russian control were not forced to serve in the military. When the requirements changed in 1916, Uzbeks who were already dissatisfied with their political and economic

A family of ethnic Russian settlers outside their home in Russian Turkestan, late 19th century. As Russia's empire expanded into Central Asia, the czars encouraged Russians to immigrate to the area. This soon led to ethnic unrest between the newcomers and native Turkic peoples such as the Uzbeks.

situation became even angrier. Several violent demonstrations took place, and the Russians responded with increasingly harsh measures.

When the Bolsheviks, members of the extremist branch of the Russian Social Democratic Worker's Party that supported the Communist theories of Vladimir Lenin, launched the Russian Revolution in St. Petersburg in 1917, demonstrations also broke out in Tashkent. The city's administration was removed, but it was not replaced by Muslim Uzbeks; instead, a new Soviet Communist power assumed control.

The remaining Jadidist leaders and other rebels made an unsuccessful attempt to establish an ***autonomous*** government in Kokand. The Bolsheviks responded by sending Russian troops to the city. Thousands of people died in the ensuing battle. Around the same time, a second rebellion, which became known as the Basmachi revolt, began. The decade-long guerrilla war ultimately split the Jadidists: some joined the rebels, while others fought alongside the Communists.

Other uprisings were suppressed in the cities of Namangan and Andizhan. The Soviets were victorious in battles for Bukhara and Khiva, resulting in the establishment of the People's Republic of Bukhara and the People's Republic of Khwarazm, the latter headquartered in Khiva. Eventually, the Basmachi rebels were defeated everywhere.

In the early years of Soviet rule, the ideals of communism, together with promises of political autonomy, won many converts from among the local population. It is not difficult to see why people who have been living in poverty and struggling for a long time to achieve a more successful life would be attracted to communism. After all, Communist theory promises that wealth will be shared equally among all members of society, rather than going overwhelmingly to a small upper class. And in theory, the Soviet Union as it evolved granted a substantial degree of autonomy to its largely ethnically based republics—including the right to secede, if the people so desired—which held appeal for nationalists. Yet the republics' political autonomy, along with the promised economic equality, was illusory, and over the years Soviet leaders took various measures that further alienated Uzbeks and other Central Asian peoples.

In 1918 some of the territory that is now Uzbekistan was made part of the Autonomous Soviet Socialist Republic of Turkestan. Two years later, the Soviet republics of Bukhara and Khwarazm were established.

Under Lenin and his successor, Joseph Stalin, the Soviet Union imposed several significant changes on traditional Central Asian society.

For example, the **Cyrillic** alphabet replaced the Arabic alphabet as the Turkic script. Literacy campaigns were initiated, as were efforts to improve the circumstances of Muslim women by, among other measures, setting a minimum age at which girls could be married and eliminating the practice of veiling women's faces.

In 1924 Joseph Stalin, who came to power in the Soviet Union upon Lenin's death that same year, delineated new borders in Central Asia, establishing the Uzbek Soviet Socialist Republic (UzSSR) and the Karakalpak Autonomous Region. (The latter would become part of Uzbekistan in 1936.) These territorial entities encompassed a large region south of the Aral Sea, including present-day Uzbekistan and Tajikistan. In 1929 the Tajik Soviet Socialist Republic was separated from the UzSSR. In drawing borders, Stalin—one of history's most manipulative and ruthless leaders—explicitly sought to divide ethnic groups and thereby thwart potential nationalist movements. He also eliminated suspected national-ists, as well as possible rivals for power, through **political purges**. In the UzSSR, many top leaders were executed; luckier ones merely suffered internal exile (a fate they shared with numerous other Uzbeks from all walks of life). Either way, during the late 1920s and 1930s Stalin replaced virtually all the existing Uzbek leaders with people whose loyalty he believed was more certain.

Under the new economic system instituted by the Soviets, the govern-ment owned all land and buildings, determined who could use land and for what purpose, and decided where people could live. By the late 1930s, most agricultural land in Uzbekistan had been taken from individuals and gathered into collective farms. On these huge collectives—which were worked by many people under the supervision of Communist Party offi-cials—food crops were largely replaced by cotton. This policy continued to draw from the dwindling local food supply as the government reserved more and more land for cotton production.

World War II (1939–1945) saw dramatic population shifts in Uzbekistan. After Germany launched a surprise invasion of the Soviet Union in 1941, Stalin moved many key industries to Uzbekistan and the other Central Asian republics, to protect them from German attack. And with the transfer of these industries came a massive influx of Russian workers, which again caused many native Uzbeks to feel their way of life threatened. In 1944, even as the war with Germany continued, Stalin ordered the deportation of the Crimea's Tatars—about 200,000 people in all—to Uzbekistan. The Soviet dictator alleged—falsely, according to most historians—that the Tatars had collaborated with the Germans after Germany overran the strategic peninsula in 1941.

Farmers plant cotton on a collective farm in the Uzbek Soviet Socialist Republic, circa 1935. Although many Uzbeks opposed collectivization and other Soviet policies, they were powerless to resist Stalin's totalitarian regime.

After a power struggle that followed Stalin's death in 1953, Nikita Khrushchev emerged as the top Soviet leader. Khrushchev's rule was less repressive than that of his predecessor, and some Uzbeks who had been exiled were allowed to return to their homeland. Also, increasing numbers of Uzbeks became Communist Party members, opening up avenues for them to gain political and social status under the Soviet system—though to do so they had to reject many aspects of their traditional culture. Finally, some of the borders of Central Asian countries were redrawn.

In 1959 Sharaf Rashidov became the first secretary of the Uzbekistan Communist Party, a position he retained for 23 years. In this powerful role, Rashidov was able to grant leadership jobs in the government of Uzbekistan to relatives and friends. He also paid liberal bribes to superiors in the central government of the Soviet Union, who looked the other way as Rashidov appropriated Uzbekistan's resources for his own enrichment and routinely fabricated cotton production numbers. After the death, in late 1982, of longtime Soviet leader Leonid Brezhnev—who had tolerated Rashidov's corruption—Moscow began scrutinizing the situation in Uzbekistan. In the years that followed, Rashidov, who died in 1983, was denounced; an investigation and subsequent trials exposed widespread corruption, particularly with regard to the cotton industry, among Uzbekistan's government and Communist Party elites; and Moscow launched a massive political purge that swept away Rashidov's associates.

Independence

While corruption had been rampant during Rashidov's tenure, many Uzbekistanis regarded the Soviet government's response as heavy-handed, and a backlash ensued. Anti-Communist and anti-Russian sentiment in Uzbekistan rose. And cotton remained a source of friction: pressures to actually meet production quotas led to the conversion of more land to cotton cultivation, thereby bringing food and water shortages, reduced water quality, and additional environmental problems.

The Soviet Union itself was foundering when Mikhail Gorbachev became its leader in 1985. To revive the crumbling Soviet economy and restore legitimacy to the Communist government, Gorbachev instituted a set of policies dubbed **perestroika** ("restructuring"), which referred to governmental and economic reform, and **glasnost** ("openness"), which basically entailed allowing a greater degree of free speech and a freer news media. In Uzbekistan (as elsewhere in the Soviet Union) glasnost emboldened opponents of the government, who began expressing their criticisms publicly. And this may have had the opposite effect of what Gorbachev had intended, fueling rather than defusing discontent with Moscow.

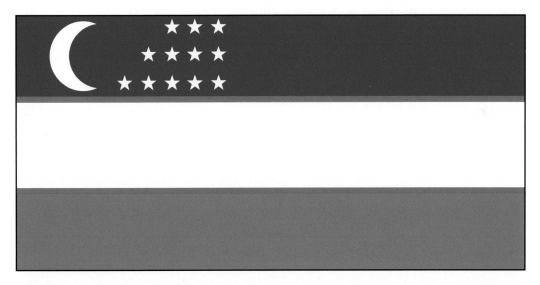

Uzbekistan's flag—adopted November 18, 1991—features three equal horizontal bands, separated by two thin red stripes. The blue band represents sky and water and recalls the banner of Timur, the white band stands for peace, and the green band symbolizes nature. The crescent moon, a traditional symbol of Islam, is also meant to represent Uzbekistan's independence and hopeful future, while the 12 stars stand for the months of the year.

In 1989 Islam Karimov was appointed first secretary of the Communist Party of Uzbekistan, making him the republic's most powerful leader. Karimov sought more control over local affairs, and Gorbachev's reforms permitted some latitude. The Communist Party of Uzbekistan declared political and economic **sovereignty** in 1990, and Karimov became president.

In August of the following year, hard-line Communist opponents of Gorbachev launched a **coup** attempt against the Soviet leader in Moscow. Although the plotters abandoned their takeover within three days and Gorbachev was restored to power, the Soviet Union would officially be dissolved by the end of the year. In December it was replaced by the Commonwealth of Independent States, a loose federation made up of 10 former Soviet republics, including Uzbekistan (as of early 2005, CIS membership had expanded to a dozen states). Uzbekistan had declared its independence less than two weeks after the coup attempt, on August 31, 1991.

Although Soviet-style communism had been swept away, members of the Communist Party of Uzbekistan who held control before independence—most prominently Islam Karimov—retained their power. And Karimov continued to rule in a manner reminiscent of the pre-Gorbachev

Karakalpak remains an autonomous republic with its own constitution, adopted in 1993. It also has its own flag, national anthem, and capital city, Nukus. Between 1.5 and 2 million people—mostly Karakalpaks and Uzbeks—live in this area, which has been devastated both environmentally and economically by the shrinking of the Aral Sea. The Karakalpak name stems from a specific type of hat the people traditionally wore (*kara* means "black" and *kalpak* means "hat").

Soviet Communist leaders: he did not tolerate dissent; he used strong-arm tactics and the state apparatus to eliminate opponents; and he maintained tight control over the news media. Elections were mere formalities rather than democratic contests. In December 1991 Karimov was elected the first president of independent Uzbekistan, but most opposition candidates had been excluded from the ballot. After banning the largest opposition parties and jailing many of his opponents for alleged treasonous activities, Karimov manipulated a 1995 referendum to extend his term in office for an additional five years. In 2000 he won another five-year presidential term in elections deemed unfair by international observers. Two years later, in another much-criticized referendum, he won approval to extend the presidential term to seven years.

As head of the Communist Party in the UzSSR, Islam Karimov was in an ideal position to take power when Uzbekistan declared its independence in August 1991.

Ongoing Challenges

Uzbekistan has faced many challenges as an independent nation, including border disputes. Some of these disagreements can be attributed to border decisions made in the 1950s. Uzbekistan claims the borders drawn in the 1920s have precedence over those drawn in the 1950s, which were never approved by the Soviet Union's legislature. Kyrgyzstan, on the other hand, adheres to the more recent borders.

At a bus stop in Tashkent, a young Muslim man distributes religious literature, an activity banned by the Karimov government. While Islamic terrorism is a legitimate cause for concern in Uzbekistan, many analysts believe
the regime's restrictions on religious activity are driving even moderate
Muslims toward extremism.

Uzbekistan has also had disagreements with Kyrgyzstan regarding
three Uzbek *enclaves* that lie within the southern region of that Central
Asian neighbor. Pockets of Uzbeks have lived in Kyrgyzstan (and
Tajikistan) for decades. In most cases, these groups never actually left
their homeland, but were separated from it by the Stalin-ordered republic
divisions of 1924 and 1929. Today, Uzbeks make up more than 10 percent
of Kyrgyzstan's population, and the government of Uzbekistan has made
claims to the lands connecting each of the ethnic Uzbek enclaves in
Kyrgyzstan with Uzbekistan.

Islamic extremism is another problem confronting Uzbekistan. Muslim terrorist organizations such as the Islamic Movement of Uzbekistan (also known as the Islamic Party of Turkestan) have been involved in a variety of violent incidents, including car bombings and kidnappings. Extremists have been able to slip easily across Central Asia's porous borders, and the region's many rugged and isolated areas hinder attempts by the authorities to root out terrorist groups.

Uzbekistan now sees Russia as an important ally in its battle against Islamic extremism. The two countries have signed military agreements, and their troops fought together in support of the government of Tajikistan in that country's 1992–1997 civil war against militant Islamists. The Shanghai Cooperation Organization (SCO), composed of Uzbekistan, Russia, China, Kyrgyzstan, Tajikistan, and Kazakhstan, has established a regional antiterrorist center in Tashkent.

But some observers believe that neither international cooperation nor increased border security will solve Uzbekistan's problems with Islamic extremism. The reason, they say, is that domestic conditions and government policies—including economic hardship, political oppression, and restrictions on religious practice—are attracting desperate Uzbekistanis to militant forms of Islam. Until those issues are addressed, critics argue, incidents such as the series of bombings and shootings that rocked Tashkent in 2004 are likely to be repeated.

"They say that it was another case of international terror . . . but I think that the main cause of the [2004] attacks is here," declared Craig Murray, Great Britain's ambassador to Uzbekistan. "The worst Soviet features such as secret police, censorship, torture in prisons are still in place here."

Islam, practiced by nearly 90 percent of the population, is Uzbekistan's dominant religion. These Muslims are participating in Friday prayers at a state-operated mosque in Margilan.

4

The Economy, Politics, and Religion

The Soviet Union—and hence its constituent republics such as Uzbekistan—had what is referred to as a command economy. Under this system, central government planners determined which goods would be produced, in what quantities, and at which locations, and then gave **subsidies** to various business entities (often state-owned enterprises) to produce the goods. Production goals, as well as the allocation of resources needed to meet those goals, were typically set in five-year economic plans; the government also established the wages of workers and the prices of the goods produced. The Soviet economic system was plagued by massive inefficiency and chronic shortages of consumer goods, but it guaranteed full employment for workers and prevented price fluctuations.

Since the breakup of the Soviet Union, Uzbekistan has been under international pressure to make the transition from a command economy to a **market economy**. In the latter system, market forces such as supply and demand and competition—rather than the government—largely determine what is produced, by whom, and how, as well as how much workers are paid and how much goods cost.

Since independence, Uzbekistan's movement toward a market economy has been halting at best. By and large, the Karimov government has sought to maintain control of business decisions, and in the immediate post-Soviet period its grip on production and prices actually tightened. While some measures have since been introduced to open up the country to much-needed foreign investment, in most cases the manner in which these measures have been implemented has worked against that goal. The reluctance of Uzbekistan's leaders to embrace a market economy, which has cost the country opportunities for economic development, may have several explanations. On the one hand, maintaining economic control is a means of perpetuating political control—which many analysts believe is President Karimov's primary objective. On the other hand, there are real dangers to a rapid transition from a command economy to a market economy. These dangers range from a spike in unemployment to complete economic collapse—and the experience in Russia was closer to the latter.

Economic Challenges

In addition to the absence of political reform—which has discouraged foreign investment and development loans—Uzbekistan confronts a variety of barriers to economic progress. One is geography. As a doubly landlocked nation, Uzbekistan lacks access to ports, making the transportation of goods more difficult and expensive. The country also lacks a modern

The Economy of Uzbekistan

Gross domestic product (GDP*): $43.99 billion (2004 est.)

GDP per capita: $1,700 (2004 est.)

Inflation: 13.1% (2004 est.)

Natural resources: natural gas, petroleum, coal, gold, uranium, silver, copper, lead, zinc, tungsten, molybdenum

Agriculture (38% of GDP): cotton, vegetables, fruits, grains, livestock

Industry (26.3% of GDP): textiles, food processing, machine building, metallurgy, natural gas, chemicals

Services (35.7% of GDP): government, education, health, banking

Foreign trade:

Imports—$2.31 billion: machinery and equipment, foodstuffs, chemicals, metals

Exports—$2.83 billion: cotton, gold, energy products, mineral fertilizers, ferrous metals, textiles, food products, automobiles (2004 est.)

Currency exchange rate: 1,047 Uzbekistan sums = U.S. $1 (November 2004)

*GDP, or gross domestic product, is the total value of goods and services produced in a country annually (here estimated using the purchasing power parity method).

All figures are 2003 estimates unless otherwise noted.

Sources: CIA World Factbook, 2004; Bloomberg.com.

infrastructure to support new businesses. Much of its telephone system, highways, and railroads need to be upgraded. While construction has taken place on some of the major roads, many less-traveled roads are in serious need of repair. Antiquated factory equipment (for example, equipment for baking and packaging bread that is more than 50 years old) slows production, to say nothing of the difficulty in obtaining replacement parts.

Using an antiquated Soviet-era reaping machine, farmhands harvest wheat in a field in Djizak. Because much of the agricultural and industrial equipment used in Uzbekistan dates from the 1950s, the country's economy is plagued by production inefficiencies.

Until recently, Uzbekistan's economy faced a major stumbling block because it did not have a "convertible currency"—money that can be easily and lawfully exchanged for another form of money. Uzbekistan introduced its own currency, the sum-kupon, in 1993. In 1994 the sum-kupon was replaced by the sum, which has since fallen in value and buying power. When the currency was first introduced, one U.S. dollar was worth 25 sums; by late 2004 the dollar was trading for about 1,050 sums. While the sum has gotten weaker, the cost of food and other necessities has risen. This situation has caused great hardship for Uzbekistanis.

In large part because the government has continued to cling to a command economy, Uzbekistan's unemployment rate has remained very low—an estimated 0.5 percent in 2003. But **underemployment** is a major problem, affecting as many as one in five workers. Compounding these problems is Uzbekistan's young population: approximately 60 percent of the country's people are under the age of 25. Educating, training, and creating jobs for all the young people entering the workforce is, and will continue to be, an enormous challenge for the government.

Economic Sectors

Agriculture continues to be a major foundation of Uzbekistan's economy. It employs more than 4 in 10 of the country's workers and accounts for an estimated 38 percent of gross domestic product, or GDP. (GDP, a primary measure of economic activity, is the total value of goods and services produced in a country annually.)

Within the agricultural sector, cotton is still king: Uzbekistan remains one of the world's largest exporters of the crop known as "white gold." Despite its continuing importance as a cash crop, overdependence on cotton has had certain negative consequences for Uzbekistan. Decades of growing only cotton, rather than rotating crops, has exhausted the soil. Average yields per acre have declined, and the government's solution—pouring more and more fertilizers onto the land—has led to environmental degradation. Moreover, because cotton exports form such an important part of Uzbekistan's economy, the country remains vulnerable to fluctuations in world prices for the commodity. If the price of cotton on the world market declines, Uzbekistan is deprived of much-needed income. And to a large extent, Uzbekistani farmers are at the mercy of government policies that emphasize cotton production. Although the collective farms of the Soviet era have been broken up, the government still owns the land, which individual farmers lease from the government. In many areas, farmers must fulfill their government-imposed quotas on cotton or risk losing the right to farm the land. This limits the amount of

Three women unload and sort silkworm cocoons at a silk factory in Urganch. The silk industry is an important part of Uzbekistan's economy.

land the farmers can devote to cultivating other crops that might be financially attractive.

Besides cotton, some cereal grains and rice are grown in Uzbekistan for export. Many fruits and vegetables are grown for local consumption. Significant nonfood crops include jute (which is used to make twine) and tobacco.

At the bases of its mountain ranges, Uzbekistan has some rich pastureland that supports livestock (primarily cattle and sheep). Karakul sheep are among the most unusual breeds raised in Uzbekistan. Unlike other types of sheep, it is the Karakul's pelt (rather than its wool) that is used to make clothing. Although it may seem strange to think of a worm as livestock, silkworms are raised on mulberry trees in Karakalpak and the Fergana Valley, and the silk industry is a major part of Uzbekistan's economy.

Uzbekistan's industrial sector accounts for a little more than a quarter of the country's GDP. Among the notable industries are **metallurgy**, aircraft manufacturing, machine building, natural gas, and textiles. The world's largest cotton processing plant is located in Tashkent, but Uzbekistan still sends most of its cotton to Russia for processing. Additional industries include the manufacture of cement and other building materials, chemicals, and fertilizers. The making of traditional Uzbek crafts—which was discouraged under early Russian rule—recently has been enjoying a comeback. Today artisans dye silk, weave carpets, and make pottery. These handcrafted items are now being sold in many cities.

Many experts believe that to further develop its industrial sector, Uzbekistan would benefit from more private enterprise and less government involvement and ownership. Although the government has touted the "extremely favorable conditions" that it says have been created for foreign investment, many investors apparently are not yet convinced. Still, several foreign companies have set up significant joint ventures in Uzbekistan. Newmont Gold, a Canadian company, has invested in the extraction of Uzbekistan's gold deposits. A British firm is involved in the production of natural gas. A company from Turkey has invested in a pharmaceutical facility in Tashkent, and a corporation from South Korea has invested heavily in car manufacturing in Andizhan. Many new jobs have been created by joint ventures like these.

Uzbekistan's service sector, which employs an estimated 36 percent of the workforce, contributes roughly the same percentage to the GDP. Service workers include teachers, health-care providers, bankers, shopkeepers, and other professionals.

Overall, Uzbekistan is a poor country. Its 2003 GDP per capita—essentially each citizen's average share of the country's annual economic activity—was estimated at just $1,700, using a method that adjusts for the local cost of living. But within that average of $1,700, there is severe inequality, and that inequality has grown dramatically since independence from the Soviet Union. A recent estimate indicated that the richest 10 percent of Uzbekistan's citizens share a total of about one-third of the country's income, whereas the poorest 10 percent share slightly more than 1 percent of the wealth.

Natural Resources

Arguably the most important natural resource in an arid country like Uzbekistan is water. In addition to serving an agricultural function, water is used to produce electricity. More than 20 hydroelectric power plants operate in Uzbekistan.

Surprisingly, this desert land once had a thriving fishing industry thanks to the Aral Sea. Muynak was a fishing village located at the edge of the water, which was once filled with life. Here, generations made their living by fishing, processing the catch, and shipping the abundant food to other regions. Today, what is left of Muynak lies approximately 93 miles (150 km) from the Aral Sea. At first, the town tried to keep its ties to the sea by digging a canal linking Muynak to the water's edge, though the water kept receding. Now the decaying remains of rusty ships lie scattered on a salty desert bed that once provided a living for thousands of people in the northern part of Karakalpak. The salinity of the soil renders the land useless for farming, and it is questionable whether this sad wasteland can ever be restored.

Uzbekistan is energy self-sufficient. Significant oil fields are being tapped in the Fergana Valley, close to the border with Afghanistan, and in the south-central part of the country. It is also one of the world's top producers of natural gas. Large deposits are currently being exploited in parts of the Fergana Valley as well as in Karakalpak and the areas near Bukhara and the Turkmenistan border. During the Soviet era, pipelines were constructed to transport natural gas and oil from Central Asia to Russia, and even after the Soviet Union broke up, Russia maintained some control over the flow of these resources. In recent years, however, Uzbekistan has reserved more than two-thirds of the natural gas it produces for domestic use and sold most of the remainder to neighboring countries and Azerbaijan. And projects are under way to build new pipelines in Central Asia that bypass Russia as they send oil and natural gas out of the region.

Gold is among Uzbekistan's other mineral resources, and large deposits are currently being mined. The country also contains significant deposits of coal, copper, zinc, tungsten, lead, fluorspar, molybdenum, and uranium. Karakalpak has granite and marble, and iron ore is mined along the edge of the Fergana Valley.

Uzbekistan could potentially have a thriving tourist industry. The country is lavishly endowed with biodiversity and beautiful contrasting terrain. A vital national park system was established under the Soviets (though some of the protected lands are now under threat from poaching, the cutting of wood for fuel, and the grazing of livestock). In addition, the country has an abundance of fascinating and historically important sites, including Samarqand, Khiva, and Bukhara, which are all recognized as World Heritage sites by UNESCO (the United Nations Educational, Scientific and Cultural Organization). Many tourists would undoubtedly like to visit Uzbekistan but are discouraged by the country's reputation for administrative hassles and police harassment. As with other aspects of its economy, Uzbekistan's tourist industry will probably never reach its full potential unless significant government reforms are undertaken.

Politics and Government

Uzbekistan has the trappings of a Western-style democracy: a constitution that guarantees political and civil rights; multiparty elections; constitutionally mandated separation of powers between executive, legislative, and judicial branches. Yet few independent observers would say that Uzbekistan enjoys a democratic form of government in any meaningful sense. Since independence, Uzbekistan has been ruled dictatorially by Islam Karimov, whose critics have noted the similarities between his methods and those of the former Soviet Union's leaders.

In Uzbekistan the president—the position Karimov officially holds—is head of state and chief executive. Even aside from Karimov's extraordinary consolidation of authority, the presidency was designed to be a powerful post. As specified in Uzbekistan's 1992 constitution, the president appoints and may remove the head of government—the prime minister—as well as 10 deputy prime ministers and other cabinet members. The president also nominates judges to the highest courts and appoints and may dismiss judges to courts at the regional level or lower. In addition, the president may initiate legislation. As commander-in-chief of the armed forces, the president is empowered to appoint and dismiss top military leaders; he also has considerable authority in managing the state security apparatus, including control of appointments and dismissals. Originally, Uzbekistan's constitution spelled out a five-year term for the presidency and limited presidents to two consecutive terms. But those limitations have proved meaningless, as Karimov has effectively obtained three terms in office, and a referendum in 2002 approved amending the constitution to extend the length of the president's term to seven years.

If there is a meaningful check on the authority of Islam Karimov, analysts believe that it comes from Uzbekistan's regional clans. Leaders of these clans compete with one another for political control and seek to monopolize economic resources in a manner reminiscent of the Communist Party elite during Soviet times. In formulating policy, Karimov's regime cannot completely disregard the wishes of the regional clan heads, a situation that has important ramifications in the political and economic spheres. For example, the central government would find it difficult to fully institute a free-market economy (assuming it actually wanted to) because clan leaders would vigorously oppose such a move, which could undermine their control of profitable business enterprises.

Uzbekistan's legislature is called the Oliy Majlis (Supreme Assembly). Initially it was a one-chamber body, but the 2002 referendum that approved extension of the president's term also approved creation of a second legislative chamber, which was filled by elections in December 2004. The new upper house of the Oliy Majlis consists of 100 senators, 84 of them chosen by regional councils and the remaining 16 appointed by the president. The lower house of Uzbekistan's parliament consists of 120 deputies, each representing a single district and elected by popular vote. All members of the Oliy Majlis serve five-year terms.

Islam Karimov casts his ballot during a 2002 referendum to extend the length of his term as president. Karimov, Uzbekistan's only president, has concentrated political power is his own hands.

In theory, the Oliy Majlis resembles other parliaments throughout the world—exercising primary lawmaking responsibility in Uzbekistan and approving various appointments and initiatives of the president. In practice, however, it has been little more than a rubber stamp for the Karimov regime, which controls the political process at all levels. The upper house of the Oliy Majlis is not elected by popular vote, but even in the lower house, which is, running for a seat is nearly impossible without the nomination of a registered political party. And it is the Ministry of Justice that registers political parties. Before the December 2004 legislative elections, there were only five registered political parties, and all were allies of President Karimov. In addition to the registration barrier, potential opposition parties face official harassment as well as government control of the media.

Most outside observers believe that, like its legislature, Uzbekistan's judicial system falls considerably short of being independent. For example, an Amnesty International press release in November 2003 reported, "Uzbekistan's flawed criminal justice system provides fertile ground for miscarriages of justice and executions due to judicial error or grossly unfair trials." According to independent advocacy groups and family members of the convicted, thousands of political dissidents—especially Muslims who practice their religion outside state-approved mosques—have been arrested on vague charges of "subversion" or "anti-state activities" and received long prison terms after undergoing unfair trials. And the United Nations has said that in Uzbekistan's justice system, torture is "institutionalized, systematic, and rampant."

Administratively, Uzbekstan is divided into 12 provinces, each called a *viloyat*, in addition to the Karakalpak Autonomous Republic. The *viloyatlar* (plural form of *viloyat*) are Andizhan, Bukhara, Dzhizak, Fergana, Kashka-Darya, Khorezm, Namangan, Navoi, Samarqand, Surkhandarya, Syr Dar'ya, and Tashkent. The administrative government of each province is called the *hokimiat* and is led by a *hokim* (mayor), who is appointed by the president.

The strong hand of the central government reaches down from the capital in Tashkent into the heart of local communities through their *mahalla* committees. The *mahalla*, meaning "neighborhood" or "community," is an institution dating back as far as the 11th century. Traditionally, it was composed of several hundred people who lived in the same area and shared the same ethnicity or profession, with elders providing leadership and guidance. *Mahalla* activities frequently centered on the neighborhood mosque and often involved local celebrations and Islamic traditions. The Karimov regime has heavily promoted *mahallas*—there are today an estimated 12,000 throughout the country—ostensibly because they represent an important element of Uzbek culture, though clearly the government has used *mahalla* committees as a means of monitoring the populace and suppressing dissent.

Muhammad Salih, the leader of the nationalist Erk ("Freedom") movement in Uzbekistan, sits in a jail in Prague, Czech Republic, where he was briefly detained at the request of Uzbekistan's government. The Karimov regime, which ruthlessly suppresses dissent, forced Salih to leave Uzbekistan by accusing him of involvement in Islamist terrorist activities, even though Erk is a secular movement.

Mahalla leaders are generally elected, but they must be approved by the *hokim,* and the chairman of the *mahalla* is usually appointed by the *hokimiat.* Additionally, the Posbon Law, adopted in 1999, has created the new position of the *posbon* (neighborhood guardian) within the *mahalla.* These individuals are paid by the government and work with the local police. Through them, the government can now obtain reports of suspicious behavior among neighborhood residents.

Religion

Islam—first introduced to Central Asia in the seventh century by Arabs—has had a profound influence on the history and culture of Uzbekistan, as the country's thousands of mosques attest. Today close to 90 percent of the people of Uzbekistan are Muslims, with the vast majority belonging to the orthodox Sunni branch of Islam. In addition to Shia Muslims, Uzbekistan's religious minorities include members of the Russian Orthodox Church as well as a very small number of other Christians, Jews, Jehovah's Witnesses, and Buddhists.

Uzbekistan's Muslims are among the more than 1 billion adherents of Islam worldwide. The so-called five pillars of Islam define the basic obligations of the faithful: *Shahada*, a profession of faith ("There is no God but Allah, and Muhammad is His prophet"); daily prayer at five specified times; charity to the poor; fasting between dawn and dusk during the holy month of Ramadan; and hajj, a pilgrimage to Mecca (the birthplace of Muhammad), which all Muslims try to make at least once in their lifetime.

Soviet communism was expressly atheistic, and the Soviet government suppressed religion throughout the USSR. But Islam had been a vital part of the Uzbekistani culture for centuries, and not even the coercive power of the state could make it disappear. In the late 1940s, the Soviet government decided to place the Muslims of Central Asia under an officially sanctioned religious authority called the *Muftiyat*.

In the early 1980s, only about 80 mosques operated openly in Uzbekistan, but during the era of reform under Mikhail Gorbachev, previously secret mosques began to surface. When the lid of Communist oppression was lifted with the breakup of the Soviet Union, a reawakening of religious sentiment occurred among the Uzbekistani population. More than 1,000 mosques were soon operating in the Fergana Valley

Citizens accused of involvement in a string of deadly blasts and shoot-outs with police in early 2004 sit in a cage during their trial at the Supreme Court of Uzbekistan in Tashkent. Independent observers have characterized Uzbekistan's judicial system as "flawed" and "grossly unfair," and human rights abuses are said to be commonplace.

alone. Middle Eastern countries have provided funding for the restoration of old mosques and the building of new ones. There are also increasing numbers of schools for Islamic instruction, and more of Uzbekistan's people are participating in the hajj to Mecca.

In general, Muslims in Central Asia, including Uzbekistan, tend to be more tolerant and less restrictive than their co-religionists in other parts of the Islamic world, such as Iran and Saudi Arabia. This may be attributable to the historically moderating influence of Sufism on Islamic practice in the region.

For its part, the Karimov regime has been wary of Uzbekistan's Islamic revival. Of particular concern are radical fundamentalist groups, such as the Islamic Movement of Uzbekistan, which advocates the overthrow of the Karimov government and its replacement with a conservative Islamic regime. Perhaps more dangerous in the long run, even though it does not explicitly promote violence, is Hizb ut-Tahrir. Founded in the early 1950s in Saudi Arabia and East Jerusalem, Hizb ut-Tahrir is now a global organization thought to operate in more than 40 countries. It came to Uzbekistan in 1995 and, a decade later, is believed to have at least 15,000 supporters there. Hizb ut-Tahrir's goal is to establish an Islamic caliphate, or political dominion, governed by *Sharia* (Islamic law). Such a caliphate would include Uzbekistan and the rest of Central Asia. The group has been vague about how it plans to create a caliphate, but many analysts suspect that a violent revolution would be required.

The government of Uzbekistan has taken a variety of steps—many of them quite repressive—to contain this threat. But in the view of many analysts, the harshness of the government response may be backfiring, increasing rather than diminishing the appeal of militant Islam.

Central to the Karimov government's efforts to contain Muslim fundamentalism has been the promotion of an Islamic sect known as the Naqshbandi order. Naqshbandis, whose sect has roots in Zoroastrianism, follow the Muslim mystical tradition known as Sufism. Since their focus is on cultivating a personal relationship with God, they tend to be less concerned with the political dimensions of Islam and hence less of a threat to the government. But the government of Uzbekistan has gone well beyond mere promotion of a moderate Islamic sect. In 1998 it passed a law greatly restricting religious practice. Among other provisions, the law prohibited Muslims from worshiping in mosques not approved by and registered with the government, or even from wearing religious dress in public (Uzbekistani exiles have said that men are routinely picked up and interrogated simply for wearing a beard). Uzbekistan's Council of Religious Affairs is now responsible for authorizing religions before they can be practiced. In addition, sermons are monitored; religious leaders who do not preach an approved version of Islam are replaced, or their mosques are closed. It is also illegal to possess certain religious literature (including some Christian writings).

The Karimov government is confronting a jihad, or holy war, from Muslim extremists. However, under the guise of fighting terrorism, the government has targeted thousands of moderate Muslims for repression, according to a variety of news, human rights, and diplomatic sources. Harassment, arbitrary detention, and torture are widespread, these sources claim. Ultimately, Western analysts worry, the government crackdown may play into the hands of the Muslim extremists.

Uzbek girls walk down a street in Bukhara. The Uzbeks are the largest ethnic group in the country, making up four-fifths of the population.

5

the People

The vast majority of Uzbekistan's population lives in densely populated rural areas. For people living in countries like the United States and Canada, "densely populated" and "rural area" are terms that are rarely used together. However, the settlements in Uzbekistan are the product of natural circumstances: the country's extensive desert terrain demands that people living in rural areas congregate near water in crowded communities.

Uzbekistan is a diverse country. While native Uzbeks, who are of Turkic, Persian, and Mongolian descent, make up a large majority of the population (80 percent), there are also dozens of minority groups. The largest of these groups are the Russians (though thousands of ethnic Russians left Uzbekistan after independence) and the Tajiks. Russian is a common language in multi-ethnic areas, and Tajik, a language that is similar to Farsi, is widely used in Bukhara and Samarqand, two cities with Tajik majorities.

Family Life

Uzbekistani society is very traditional, with family playing a central role for most people. Generosity and hospitality are greatly valued in Uzbekistan, and even families that do not have much money themselves—which includes most of the country—take pride in opening their doors and extending a warm welcome to visitors.

Roles within the family are clearly defined. Conservative Islamic roots dictate that the father is the unquestioned head of the family. All elderly family members have high positions within the family hierarchy and are given great respect by the children. There are different ways of addressing people depending upon their age and position in the family. At mealtimes, for example, more respected individuals may not be spoken to directly. Thus a young girl might speak to her mother rather than directly addressing her father.

When men have free time away from family and jobs, they often spend it seated around low tables in *chaikhanas* (teahouses). A lot of interaction takes place in these traditional gathering places, where tea is served in a *piola* (a cup without handles) and is often accompanied by an assortment of sweets.

Men and women do most of their shopping in bazaars. Many people earn their livelihood as craftspeople or vendors at these collections of open-air shops, which provide a lively blend of sounds, colors, and aromas along with a wide variety of merchandise. Bazaars are an ancient tradition and afford a place for social activity as well as shopping. All of a family's day-to-day needs, from fresh fruits and vegetables to spices, clothing, embroidery, ceramics, knives, and flowers, can be purchased in bazaar shops.

Three Uzbek men enjoy flatbread, tea, and conversation at a *chaikhana* in Samarqand.

Even in the 21st century, arranged marriages are quite common in Uzbekistan, especially in rural areas. Sometimes, however, the young man and woman have input; after meeting and falling in love, they may ask their respective parents to get together and arrange a marriage. Women often marry between the ages of 19 and 22, and sisters traditionally marry in birth order. A woman who has reached the age of 25 and is still not married may be considered an "old maid." Men are often a year or two older than their brides.

It is common for married couples to live with the groom's parents, and the bride is expected to assume all household chores. When the next son in the family marries, however, the eldest son and his wife may move out and establish their own household.

Rural families are usually large. Most include four or five children, and it is not uncommon to have twice that number. Islam traditionally allowed a man to have up to four wives at the same time, but polygamy was outlawed during the Soviet era. While having multiple wives remains illegal in Uzbekistan, observers have noted that the practice is on the rise. Typically, polygamous unions involve an older, wealthier man whose second wife comes from a poor family with limited prospects; in most cases the man maintains separate households for each of his wives.

Family Meals

Those curious about Uzbekistani culture can gain some understanding of its family hierarchy by observing the traditional meal, which is typically served on a low table, with family members seated directly on the floor

In Uzbekistan, families traditionally eat their meals while seated on the floor around a low table.

Several Uzbek traditions and superstitions involve bread, which many people consider a sacred food. It is unlucky to place bread upside-down, and it should never be set on the ground. A piece of bread is sometimes placed under the heads of newborns as a symbol that they will lead a long life and always have what they need. When babies first begin to walk, their parents may place a little piece of bread on their legs to bless their path in life. If a son should go to war, his mother may break a round of bread into two pieces, sending one piece with her son. By holding on to the other piece and not eating it, she hopes to keep him safe.

or on pillows or rugs as they eat. The eldest family member is usually seated farthest from the door. This person may say a prayer before and after the meal. Younger members of the family look after the needs of the elders, filling their cups with tea and passing food to them as needed. Most cooking and other household tasks are the responsibility of a daughter-in-law or the oldest daughter.

Plov, a kind of rice pilaf, is one of Uzbekistan's traditional foods. It is usually made with an assortment of vegetables and meat. A sweeter version of this dish includes dried fruits such as raisins or apricots. *Shashlik* (shish kebab) is a favorite way to prepare meat, especially mutton. Meat pastries are also popular, and a round, flat bread called *non* is served at every meal. Tea, called *chai*, is the most common beverage in Uzbekistan, and green tea is usually favored over black tea. Vodka and wine are also consumed.

Single-family homes often have a *hovli* (courtyard) where grapevines and fruit trees are planted. Sometimes families eat and even sleep in this courtyard. Many Uzbeks, particularly those living in rural areas, have gardens. When fruits and vegetables are abundant, they are canned for use during other times of the year.

Traditional Dress, Arts, and Crafts

Blue jeans, suits, skirts, and all manner of Western clothing are worn in the cities of Uzbekistan, but many people still display their rich cultural heritage by wearing more traditional dress. Women wear tunic-like dresses over pants; usually, these garments are made of rainbow-colored silk. Men wear shirts and pants and, in the winter, long coats tied closed with belts or sashes. Many men also wear traditional skullcaps; these are usually black with white embroidered designs of objects such as peppers or almonds (a symbol of happiness in the Uzbek culture). The patterns on a skullcap designate the man's home region.

Because the government is trying to preserve the artistic heritage of Uzbekistan, it is now illegal to export crafts and art pieces that are more than 100 years old. However, highly skilled craftspeople have recently begun using the old methods to make new items. Karakalpak and Samarqand are renowned for beautiful rugs. The Fergana Valley and Khiva are known for a distinctive style of blue-and-white ceramics. Copper engraving has been a specialty of Tashkent, Bukhara, Khiva, and Samarqand since the days of the Silk Road. Craftspeople still make items such as trays and teapots in these cities. Wood carving, calligraphy, embroidery, and the painting of miniatures are other important crafts.

Stringed instruments and flutes are among the instruments used to produce Uzbekistan's traditional music. Complicated rhythms and melodies form a sophisticated music much like that heard in the neighboring Middle East. Sometimes these intricate rhythms are anchored with the beat of a *doira* (flat drum). Occasionally, a six-foot-long horn joins the ensemble. Tashkent artist Monajat Yultchieva is one of the

Traditional dancers performing in the Bukhara style, which involves wrist bells and quick movements.

best-known singers of traditional music. Two popular musical groups in Uzbekistan today are a girl's trio called Sitora and a male duo called Dado.

Certain Uzbek dance forms predate the sixth century A.D. They focus on the upper body, with the arms, hands, and face used to express emotions. Spinning and turning are important motions, and sometimes the performer kneels during the dance. There are three styles of traditional dance, corresponding with the ancient areas of Bukhara, Khiva, or the Fergana Valley. The dances differ in costume and movement. The Bukhara and Khiva styles often involve the use of wrist bells. In addition, the Khiva style is distinguished by its quivering motions, though it is mostly performed with the dancer's feet remaining stationary. The vigorous Bukhara style involves much more movement, while the Fergana style has been described as soft and elegant. Qizlarhon Dustmuhamedova is one of the country's most famous female traditional dancers and has performed all these styles in Europe, the Middle East, and the United States.

Language and Education

Uzbek became the official language of Uzbekistan in 1990. Its roots lie in Chagatai, an extinct Turkic language that was once spoken in parts of Central Asia. Uzbek is also related to a language called Uygur, a Turkic tongue still spoken by several million people in Central Asia, the Middle East, and the Xinjiang Uygur Autonomous Region of China. Many people in Uzbekistan—government leaders and students, in particular—also speak Russian, and Uzbek speech is often sprinkled with terms borrowed from Russian as well as Persian. In Bukhara and Samarqand a large segment of the population speaks Tajik.

The Soviet government forced the Cyrillic alphabet (which is used in Russia) on Uzbekistan, but use of the Latin script has been returning since

Common Uzbek Phrases with English Translations

Marhamat	Please
Rakhmat	Thank you
Hop	Yes
Yuk, janob	No, sir
Sizning ismingiz nima?	What is your name?
Necha yoshdasiz	How old are you?
Hayrli tong	Good morning
Hayrli kun	Good afternoon
Hayir	Good-bye

The right side of this sign outside the Islamic Institute in Tashkent is written in the Cyrillic and Latin alphabets, both of which are commonly used in Uzbekistan. Few Uzbeks can read Arabic, shown on the left side of the sign, but growing interest in Islam since the fall of the Soviet Union means that more people are learning the language.

independence. This change has begun with the conversion of public signs and the introduction of the Latin alphabet into the school curriculum. For older Uzbekistanis who grew up learning Cyrillic letters and the Russian language, this constitutes a major adjustment.

During the Soviet era, education was free and the school system was strong. As a result, illiteracy was virtually eliminated by 1970. Since the breakup of the Soviet Union, however, the government of Uzbekistan has not been able to continue funding education at pre-independence levels. The educational system now comes under the direction of two national agencies, the Ministry of Higher Education and the Ministry of People's Education. The Ministry of Higher Education oversees postsecondary schooling, while the other ministry oversees everything else, including vocational training.

Uzbekistan's government wants to modernize and improve the country's educational system, but this goal has run up against the burden of a

Students work on their lessons in a school near Samarqand. Since independence, Uzbekistan's government has struggled to fund the country's educational system, and computers, textbooks, and other basic tools of learning are often in short supply.

The People of Uzbekistan

Population: 26,410,416
Ethnic groups: Uzbek, 80%; Russian, 5.5%; Tajik, 5%;
  Kazakh, 3%; Karakalpak, 2.5%; Tatar, 1.5%; other,
  2.5% (1996 est.)
Age structure:
  0–14 years: 34.1%
  15–64 years: 61.1%
  65 years and over: 4.8%
Population growth rate: 1.65%
  Birth rate: 26.12 births/1,000 population
  Infant mortality rate: 71.3 deaths/1,000 live births
  Death rate: 7.95 deaths/1,000 population
Life expectancy at birth:
  total population: 64.09 years
  males: 60.67 years
  females: 67.69 years
Total fertility rate: 2.97 children born/woman
Religions: Muslim, 88% (mostly Sunnis); Eastern Orthodox,
  9%; other, 3%
Languages: Uzbek, 74.3%; Russian, 14.2%; Tajik, 4.4%;
  other, 7.1%
Literacy: 99.3% (2003 est.)

All figures are 2004 estimates unless otherwise indicated.
Source: CIA World Factbook, 2004.

rapidly expanding population of young people. Meeting the educational requirements of so many requires massive public expenditures in a country that is strapped for funds. Thousands of school buildings are in need of repair. In some schools, access to computers that are more than a decade old is considered a luxury; other schools lack even simple supplies.

School is compulsory through grade 9. Previously, children had to attend school through grade 11, but an ailing economy has forced many high school–aged students to drop out and enter the workforce, which typically involves toiling in the cotton fields.

Uzbekistan has more than 50 institutions of higher learning, but they also suffer from a lack of funds, as evidenced by a shortage of computers, library books, and laboratories. Students in Uzbekistan must pass an entrance examination in order to enter a university, but advanced education that once was free is becoming increasingly expensive, shutting out many otherwise qualified individuals.

Despite economic hardships, Uzbekistan has placed a high priority on education and is working to establish more schools, add new subjects (such as Uzbek history and literature), update textbooks, retrain teachers, and provide more vocational education. Teachers are receiving different kinds of training that are more in keeping with the changing economy. Some new schools focus on specific subject areas such as economics, ecology, or foreign languages. Certain organizations have worked to establish educational opportunities outside Uzbekistan. The Umit Foundation, for example, sent some 3,000 students abroad for undergrad and graduate education.

Health Care

Before the breakup of the Soviet Union, the central government planned and financed the health care system. Today health care falls under the direction of the Ministry of Health. When Uzbekistan joined the World Health Organization (WHO) in 1992, it adopted the WHO's Health for All policy. Since then, Uzbekistan has been trying to move toward a mixed system that utilizes both public and private health care. The government is the official provider of most coverage; however, because of a lack of government funds, many people have been forced

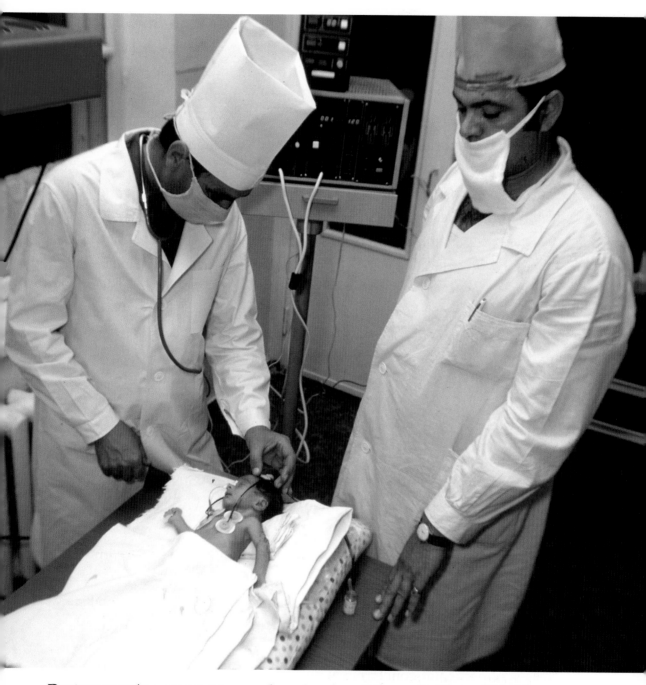

Doctors examine a premature newborn in a hospital near Bukhara. Uzbekistan faces many serious public health issues, including outdated medical facilities, shortages of qualified doctors, and high rates of certain illnesses.

to pay for their own care and medications. Large industrial companies and several government ministries offer their own health services for workers, and some even operate their own medical departments.

In 1998 the Cabinet of Ministers issued a decree to reform the health care system over the next seven years. One of the stated goals of the decree was the establishment of rural medical centers. That same year, legislation set up regional branches of the State Center for Emergency Care. These centers are funded by regional governments and by fines collected from businesses that do not comply with sanitation laws.

One of the major causes of health problems in Uzbekistan is contaminated drinking water. Much of the rural population does not have access to a monitored or regulated water supply, and wastewater in many towns does not go through a sewage-treatment facility before being released into the environment. In 2000 some of Uzbekistan's hospitals did not even have running water.

Uzbekistan's infant mortality rate is very high (more than 10 times the rate in the United States, for example). President Karimov declared 2001 the Year of Mother and Child to focus attention on this health matter. According to a study conducted that same year by UNICEF (the United Nations Children's Fund), acute respiratory infections or diarrheal diseases caused more than half of infant deaths in the country. Especially in rural areas, children who went to health centers for treatment often had more than one medical condition in need of attention. In some parts of the country, three of every four children tested were sick.

Other major health concerns in Uzbekistan include hepatitis, gallstone disease, and anemia. A lack of iodized salt has caused many people to develop goiters, which can lead to mental deficiency. Pulmonary tuberculosis is of particular concern in Karakalpak.

Despite huge challenges and the government's limited resources, some progress has been made in the area of public health. For example,

UNICEF has provided iodization machines for some salt production facilities. And in 2004 the government began requiring couples to be tested for HIV (the virus that causes AIDS), venereal diseases, and certain psychological disorders before marrying.

Sports and Games

The people of Uzbekistan enjoy a variety of sports, from ancient games to modern international competitions. Special occasions are sometimes marked by traditional games on horseback. One of these games, *bushkashi*—which is known by several other names throughout Central Asia—may have started during the 13th-century rule of Genghis Khan. The object of the game is to get a headless goat carcass over the opposing team's goal line.

Uzbekistan's Iroda Tulyaganova is among the world's best tennis players.

Kurash, a martial art and a type of upright wrestling, is also extremely popular. No one knows exactly when *kurash* began, but some historians believe it is one of the most ancient of the martial arts.

Among the more modern sports played today in Uzbekistan is tennis, a personal favorite of President Karimov's. During Russian rule the sport was vilified as a frivolous pastime of the upper class, but today tennis is actively promoted. In fact, more than 400 tennis courts have been built in Uzbekistan since the fall of the Soviet Union, and Tashkent native Iroda Tulyaganova has been ranked among the world's top 40 female players.

Festivals and Celebrations

During Soviet rule, religious festivals were banned in favor of national holidays. This was a difficult ban to enforce, however, as many of the most important celebrations among the people of Uzbekistan have religious overtones. Historically, weddings have represented important unions between families, clans, and tribes. September is a traditional month for weddings, but regardless of the time of year, they are always an occasion for great celebration, as are engagements and births. Funerals and anniversaries of deaths are also times that families come together for special rituals.

The changing of the seasons is also a cause for celebration. Novruz, which occurs on the spring equinox (when the day and night are equally long) in late March, is such a holiday. In Persian, *nov* means "new" and *ruz* means "day." Although people in Uzbekistan also celebrate New Year's Day, Novruz is more popular, and its festivities last for a week in some regions. Musicians, food vendors, craftspeople, and amusements such as carousels fill city streets. Spectators are sometimes entertained by jugglers, tightrope walkers, and performers who dance on stilts. Schools may have essay, photography, and drawing contests in honor of this special holiday.

Independence Day (September 1) is perhaps the most important recently established holiday in Uzbekistan. But the government has periodically announced other celebrations in order to foster patriotism and national unity. Such celebrations have included the 660th birthday of Timur the Great, which was observed in 1996, and the 600th birthday of the Islamic philosopher Hoja Ahror Valiy, observed in 2004.

Feasting is an important part of all celebrations. For weddings, a special *plov* is cooked by men at the home of the groom and is eaten at the bride's house. Bread that is baked for a wedding may be shaped in the form of a sun, with extra cream added to it. To commemorate the dead, men sometimes cook a different kind of *plov* that is prepared very early so it may be eaten by guests after morning prayers. Portions of the Qur'an are recited at the end of this meal. Another food that is served at special feasts is *kazi*, a sausage made from horsemeat.

Throughout Uzbekistan, the old and the new stand side by side. In this view of Tashkent, a modern hotel can be seen on the left, with the 16th-century Kukeldash Madrassa at right.

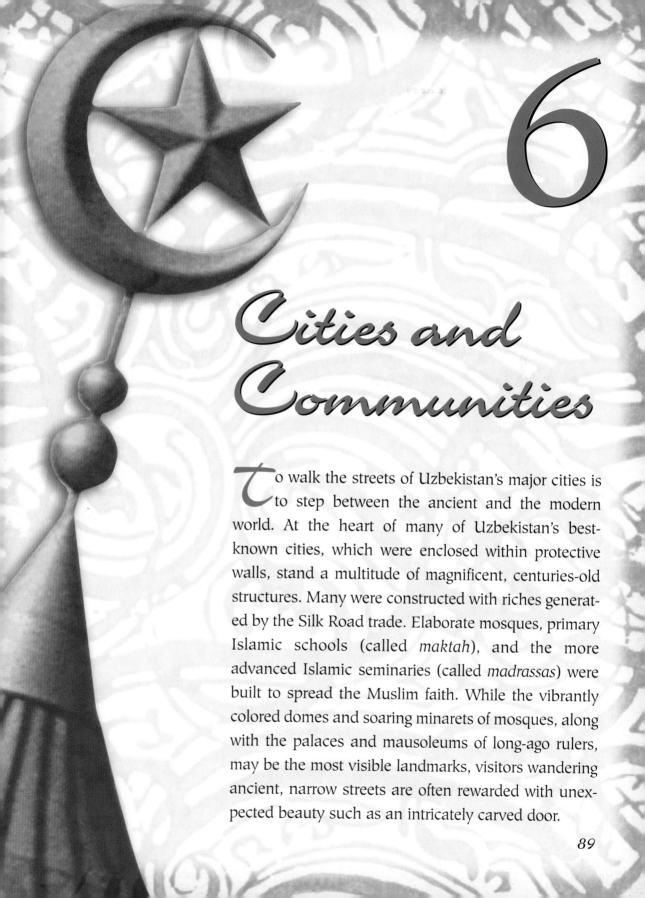

6

Cities and Communities

To walk the streets of Uzbekistan's major cities is to step between the ancient and the modern world. At the heart of many of Uzbekistan's best-known cities, which were enclosed within protective walls, stand a multitude of magnificent, centuries-old structures. Many were constructed with riches generated by the Silk Road trade. Elaborate mosques, primary Islamic schools (called *maktah*), and the more advanced Islamic seminaries (called *madrassas*) were built to spread the Muslim faith. While the vibrantly colored domes and soaring minarets of mosques, along with the palaces and mausoleums of long-ago rulers, may be the most visible landmarks, visitors wandering ancient, narrow streets are often rewarded with unexpected beauty such as an intricately carved door.

In the modern sections of Uzbekistan's cities, where hotels and high-rises have sprung up, water—that most precious of resources in this dry land—is often used to enhance the vistas. Fountains beautify many city squares, and in some cities charming brooks run parallel to tree-lined streets. Many cities have outdoor markets offering an abundance of fresh, locally grown fruits and vegetables along with countless other items.

Tashkent

The capital of Uzbekistan is located on the Chirchik River oasis in the northeastern part of the country, northwest of the Fergana Valley. In the past, Tashkent was an important trading center and a main area for the production of arts and crafts. Today, Tashkent—named by Turkic groups sometime between the 11th and 12th centuries—is a scientific and cultural center. This modern city, which had a population of about 2,295,000 in 2004, is home to the largest university in Central Asia, the Tashkent State Economic University, along with 13 other institutes of higher learning.

Tashkent is a city of contrasts. Much of the architecture shows unmistakable Soviet influence; the city was rebuilt by the Soviets after a devastating 1966 earthquake. Yet along with the 20th-century high-rise buildings are ancient structures dating to the seventh century. The district of the city where they stand, called *eski shakhar* (old city), contains narrow streets and alleys with houses constructed of mud bricks. Tashkent means "city of stone" or "the stone settlement." Visitors can view impressive madrassas that date from the 16th century, though some Islamic buildings have not survived. Some mosques were converted to factories under Russian rule; the 15th-century Jami Mosque, for example, became a sheet-metal factory.

Under the Russians, Tashkent was first the capital of the entire Russian Turkestan region (later known as Soviet Central Asia). In 1930 the city was named the capital of the Uzbek Soviet Socialist Republic.

The administrative work for the country—and in some cases, for much of the Central Asian region—takes place in this city, which now houses the Republican Commodity Exchange and the National Bank, along with the headquarters of a regional water commission.

This gateway to Central Asia is also a regional center for air and rail travel. And Tashkent boasts a subway system—the only one in Central Asia—that is modern, comfortable, and adorned with statues in its stations. In fact, the Tashkent subway system is said to rival Moscow's, which is internationally famous for its beautiful terminals.

At least nine theaters operate in Tashkent, offering entertainment that ranges from traditional Uzbek music and dancing to European operas and ballet. A total of 20 museums, including the National History Museum, Fine Arts Museum, and the Museum of Applied Arts (which alone houses approximately 30,000 examples of traditional crafts), are found in Tashkent. The city is also home to the Romanov Palace, which was built for Czar Nicholas II of Russia. People like to congregate at the many markets, including the famous Chorsu Bazaar. Hotels and restaurants serve Russian, Uzbek, and Korean foods.

Lovely shaded parks and cool fountains dot the city. In addition, several lakes and natural springs are located nearby.

The Soviet Union's second-largest statue of Vladimir Lenin once stood in Tashkent's Lenin Square. After independence, the square was renamed Independence Square, and a monument to Timur replaced the statue of the Communist leader.

Newer houses have been built on the outskirts of the city, but the majority of Tashkent's residents live in apartments. Apartment buildings are mostly of the nondescript, multi-story variety so common in the former Soviet Union. With more than 2 million residents, Tashkent was at one time the fourth-largest city in the Soviet Union (after Moscow, Leningrad, and Kiev), and it remains the largest city in Central Asia.

Tashkent is an industrial city. Products that are manufactured there include airplanes, chemicals, tobacco products, silk textiles, and furniture. Still, thousands of people are unemployed, a situation that has led to the appearance of slum-like areas.

Samarqand

Uzbekistan's second-largest city, with a population of roughly 420,000 in 2004, is one of the oldest cities in the world. Located southwest of Tashkent and just south of the Zeravshan River, fabled Samarqand has survived for almost 3,000 years. An even older city once stood on the same site. Like other cities of Uzbekistan, Samarqand has withstood wave after wave of invaders and conquerors. It thrived as a center of manufacturing and trade along the Silk Road. Arabs introduced papermaking to the city in the eighth century.

Samarqand is a city of legends. One well-known story involves Qusam ibn Abbas, a cousin of the prophet Muhammad. Qusam came to the city to preach Islam, but he was beheaded. According to the legend, he survived the ordeal by picking up his severed head and retreating to a well.

The city prospered under the Samanids but suffered greatly at the hands of Genghis Khan. Timur made Samarqand one of the greatest capitals of the world during his reign, which ended with his death in 1405. The center of Timur's capital was Registan Square, where trade was conducted, rulings were announced, and justice was meted out. Modern-day visitors are still drawn to the historic square, which is surrounded by three madrassas dating from the 15th to the 17th centuries. These magnificent structures feature luminous azure mosaics, beautifully carved marble, and glazed brick.

During the early 15th century, Samarqand became a center for science under the leadership of Timur's grandson, Ulugbek. He was very interested

Pedestrians walk through Samarqand's vast Registan Square, once the seat of Timur Lenk's power. The three buildings pictured here are the Ulugbek, Sher-Dor, and Tilla-Kari madrassas.

in astronomy and was responsible for the construction of an observatory and a school for astronomers and mathematicians. He also attracted great scientists, artists, intellectuals, and writers to the city. The oldest Muslim school in Central Asia, the Ulugbek Madrassa, was commissioned by the school's namesake in 1418. It is one of the three madrassas still standing in Registan Square.

Along with these Islamic monuments, the old city of Samarqand features historic terra-cotta brick houses like those found in Bukhara and Tashkent. Narrow alleys give way to wide, modern streets that fan out from the old city. As in days past, residents congregate at bazaars, the largest of which is located adjacent to what remains of the huge Bibi-Khanym Mosque. Constructed during the time of Timur and severely damaged during an earthquake in 1897, it was once one of the largest mosques in the world.

Another striking historic site contains the tombs of Timur's family. A jade stone, said to be the largest in the world, has been placed at Timur's tomb. This grave appears in another legend of Samarqand. According to the story, on June 22, 1941, Russian scientists were exploring Timur's grave when they unearthed a message warning that there would be severe consequences to anyone who disturbed his remains. On the same day, Nazi Germany invaded the Soviet Union.

Like other cities on the Silk Road, Samarqand fell into decline when maritime trade routes began opening up. The city became reconnected with other regions and countries at the end of the 19th century, when it was made one of the main links on the Russian-built Trans-Caspian Railway. Until 1930 it was the capital of the Uzbek Soviet Socialist Republic, and with the USSR's push to expand cotton production, Samarqand became a major collection point for that industry. Food processing and some manufacturing take place in the city today. It is also the home of several of Uzbekistan's universities.

Bukhara

First mentioned in Chinese literature in the fifth century A.D., Bukhara was established in the Zeravshan River valley to the west of Samarqand. It eventually became one of the main trading centers along the ancient Silk Road. The city's name originates from the word *vihara*, which means "monastery." Bukhara was a magnificent city under Arab control in the eighth century. Later one of its most famous residents, Sheikh Bahauddin Naqshbandi, was instrumental in the development of the mystical branch of Islam known as Sufism. Many philosophers, scientists, artists, and poets have also made Bukhara their home.

With more than 400 mosques and madrassas, Bukhara has been a center of Islamic culture. Many extravagant buildings were constructed in the city during the 9th and 10th centuries, when the Persian Samanids made it their capital. At the beginning of the 13th century, Genghis Khan and his invading army destroyed much of the city. Under the Shaybanids in the 16th century, however, Bukhara regained much of its prosperity. The largest madrassa in Central Asia, the Kukeldash Madrassa, was built in Bukhara in the 1500s.

Among Bukhara's other architectural treasures is a huge fortress known as the Ark, which served as a stronghold for rulers. The city's oldest surviving monument, considered one of Central Asia's major architectural masterpieces, is the mausoleum of Ismail Samani, a Samanid dynasty ruler. The color of the mausoleum, which was completed at the beginning of the 10th century, is said to change with the light. Another piece of striking architecture is the 12th-century Kalyan (Kalan) Mosque. At one time, the mosque's minaret, which soars 154 feet (47 meters) into the air, was the tallest building in Central Asia.

Today, people still live and work in the city's center, which looks much the same as it did two centuries ago. As in the old sections of Tashkent and Samarqand, buildings here are made of baked bricks, and the narrow alleys remain unpaved.

Government buildings, a college, and a theater are all housed

Tourists visit the ancient fortress of the khans of Bukhara, known as the Ark.

The minaret of the Kalyan Mosque in Bukhara is ornamented with decorative brickwork. This building, more than 800 years old, was once the tallest structure in Central Asia.

in the newer part of the city. Bukhara's quarter-million residents, like their compatriots elsewhere in Uzbekistan, are fond of frequenting the city's bazaars. Some of the local industries revolve around agriculture, as cotton, silk, and various fruits are grown in the surrounding area. Copper and gold ornaments are also fashioned in Bukhara. After the discovery of natural gas deposits in the area, the city became a center for gas refining.

Khiva

This ancient Silk Road city is located on the Amu Dar'ya west of Bukhara. Although one legend credits the son of the biblical patriarch Noah with its founding, the city's origins remain a mystery. Khiva is not as old as either Samarqand or Bukhara, but it was established by the time of the Arab invasion in the seventh century. Through the 12th century, Khiva remained a relatively small fortress city. By the middle of the 16th century, however, it had grown substantially. At that time, it was also a center for the slave trade. The 18th century was marked by a series of destructive invasions and wars, but the early part of the 19th century brought another period of growth to the city.

Agriculture and traditional crafts have always been leading industries in the area. Beautiful earthenware tiles, ornate carvings, and the use of marble and painting characterize many buildings. The walled inner city is called Ishan-Kala (or Itchan Kala) and is composed of well-preserved and reconstructed mosques, madrassas, palaces, and tombs. Turquoise tiles catch the eye of anyone who gazes on the Kalta Minor minaret and other buildings of the historic city. The oldest surviving part of Khiva, built in the 17th century, is called the Kunya Ark fortress; it includes a mosque, palace, arsenal, and other structures.

Four gates, one on each wall of the inner city, lead to the outer city, which is called Dishan-Kala. With a population of approximately 40,000,

A view of one of the four gates at the Kunya Ark fortress. This is the oldest surviving part of Khiva.

Khiva is rather small, but its historic core makes it one of Uzbekistan's most visited locations.

Other Cities

The city of Urganch is located just 22 miles (35 km) northeast of Khiva. At one time Urganch was a center for trade in the Khiva Khanate. Today, it is the administrative center of Khorezm Province. It is also a scientific center and home to Urganch State University. With a 2004 population of approximately 175,000, Urganch is significantly larger than its neighbor Khiva. As is common with so many cities in Uzbekistan, Urganch processes cotton (as well as rice) grown in outlying regions.

Nukus was founded to the northwest of Urganch in 1932 and became the capital of the Karakalpak Autonomous Republic in 1939. In the latter part of the 20th century, as environmental conditions in the area surrounding Nukus deteriorated, many people began moving to the city, whose population grew rapidly and soon surpassed 200,000. Nukus suffers from environmental problems of its own: winds regularly carry dangerously polluted dust and sand from the dried-up rim of the Aral Sea, and the high salt content of the city's drinking water and widespread use of pesticides are believed to be responsible for a high incidence of certain serious diseases among its residents. Attractions of Nukus include a modern art museum with an impressive collection of Soviet avant-garde art. Many of the painters and sculptors whose work is exhibited in this museum were executed or exiled in the political purges of Joseph Stalin.

The cities of Karshi, Shakhrisabz, and Termez are located south of Samarqand. Timur is said to have been particularly fond of this area in the southern part of today's Uzbekistan.

Karshi, which lies on the Kashka Dar'ya about 124 miles (200 km) from the border with Afghanistan, had an estimated 2004 population of about 232,000. The city is known for tobacco, as well as various craft items such as carpets and knives. Nearby is the Karshi-Khanabad Air Base, which the United States began using in late 2001 as part of Operation Enduring Freedom, the invasion of Afghanistan. The establishment of Karshi-Khanabad marked the first time a U.S. military base had been situated on territory that once belonged to the Soviet Union, its Cold War nemesis.

Located about 56 miles (90 km) south of Samarqand, the city of Shakhrisabz comprises one of Uzbekistan's four UNESCO World Heritage sites (the other three are in Khiva, Samarqand, and Bukhara). Shakhrisabz is where Timur was born and later built an extravagant summer palace. Fine embroidered *tubiteykas* (skullcaps), belts, and carpets are produced in this city of about 60,000, where much renovation and construction is currently taking place.

Termez (estimated 2004 population: 136,800) is located on the border between Uzbekistan and Afghanistan in an area rich in natural resources. Once one of the southernmost outposts of the Soviet Union, Termez served the supply route during the 1979 invasion of Afghanistan. The region near Termez contains deposits of natural gas, coal, and oil. Furniture, carpets, silk, sheep, cotton, rice, wheat, and other food products are produced in the area as well.

A quick tour around the Fergana Valley, located in eastern Uzbekistan, reveals several vibrant cities. Kokand, once the capital of a vast khanate and now a religious center, is located in the southwestern part of the valley, about 141 miles (228 km) southeast of Tashkent. Three hundred mosques once operated in the city. In 1917 as many as 14,000 residents of Kokand died fighting the Russians in a losing battle for freedom. The ancient city has always been on a major transportation route. Today, much of the traffic in and out of the Fergana Valley passes through Kokand, which is situated at the crossroads of two major routes (one going northwest toward Tashkent and the other heading west through Tajikistan and then back into Uzbekistan). Food, textiles, and chemicals are all produced in the area.

The old city of Margilan and the relatively new city of Fergana are located east of Kokand. Margilan, home to some 150,000 residents, has always been famous for its silk and today is the site of a large silk factory. Construction of Fergana, a city of more than 220,000 residents, began in 1877. At that time, more than 10,000 trees were planted. Although it is today an industrial city, Fergana remains very attractive. Some residents refer to it as "the Sleeping Beauty" because many people who are not from the area are unaware of its loveliness.

Andizhan is located in the far eastern part of Uzbekistan, in a province of the same name. This oil-producing city surrounded by farms had an estimated 2004 population of more than 360,000. Important businesses in Andizhan and the surrounding area include textile manufacturers, construction companies, chemical plants, and an automobile production facility, recently begun as a joint venture with Korean industrialists.

Namangan, an ancient city that lies in the northern part of the Fergana Valley, has more than 440,000 residents. The area abounds in mineral resources, including oil, copper, gold, lead, and antimony. Namangan is also home to silk, cotton, and leather industries, along with construction and fertilizer companies.

Namangan and the rest of the Fergana Valley have seen much ethnic conflict. More than 100 people died in an uprising in 1989, when Uzbeks clashed with Meskhetians (descendants of a group that was deported from Soviet Georgia in the 1940s). The valley has also seen terrorist activity and is a prime recruiting ground for the IMU and Hizb ut-Tahrir. The adopted name of one of the IMU's founders, Juma Namangani, was taken from his hometown.

Presidents Hu Jintao of China (left) and Islam Karimov participate in a joint press conference during Hu's June 2004 visit to Uzbekistan. In recent years the two countries have agreed to strengthen security and economic ties.

7

Foreign Relations

$\mathcal{T}$hroughout most of the 20th century, Uzbekistan was part of the Soviet Union. This not only meant that Uzbekistan was effectively shut off from the rest of the world, but also precluded the need for a foreign policy.

When the Soviet Union collapsed in 1991 and Uzbekistan became an independent state, it was suddenly confronted with the task of establishing relations with other countries and crafting a foreign policy to serve its national interests. Uzbekistan has sought to become an economic and political leader in Central Asia. For their part, other nations have recognized the renewed strategic importance of independent Uzbekistan.

In the 15-odd years since gaining independence,

Uzbekistan has become a member of various international and regional organizations, including the United Nations, the Organization for Security and Co-operation in Europe (OSCE), the Organization of the Islamic Conference (OIC), and the Shanghai Coooperation Organization (SCO). Uzbekistan has also participated in two programs sponsored by the North Atlantic Treaty Organization (NATO): the Partnership for Peace program and the Euro-Atlantic Partnership Council (EAPC). With other nations it has signed numerous environmental agreements, including ones regarding climate change, hazardous wastes, and endangered species.

Neighbors in Central Asia

In some ways, a sort of sibling rivalry exists between Uzbekistan and the other Central Asian countries that were formerly under Soviet domination. Much of their history is shared and they have similar needs, especially in the area of economic development. Yet they also have competing interests. One important cause for dispute is water. When more than one country shares a river, as is the case with the Syr Dar'ya, it is understandable that this valuable resource would create conflict, particularly during times of drought. Communities that are downstream also complain about the pollutants that enter rivers upstream. Uzbekistan has had occasional disputes with Kyrgyzstan, Tajikistan, and Turkmenistan regarding these issues.

Sometimes the government of Uzbekistan has resorted to rather heavy-handed tactics in the face of disagreements with its Central Asian neighbors. For example, when Kyrgyzstan in 1993 stopped using the Russian ruble as its currency—a decision that threatened to disrupt economic cooperation between the Central Asian republics—President Karimov stopped the flow of natural gas from Uzbekistan to Kyrgyzstan. He took the same course of action in 1998 because Kyrgyzstan joined the World Trade Organization. Other conflicts have developed from the intense competition over natural resources such as oil.

Despite these conflicts, the countries of Central Asia have a mutual interest in developing security and a strong regional economy. Leaders in Tashkent and the other Central Asian capitals recognize the necessity of regional cooperation if any of their respective countries hope to compete and prosper in an age of increasing globalization. Uzbekistan and Kazakhstan were the first two countries in the Commonwealth of Independent States (CIS) to conclude formal economic agreements, coordinating to establish the free flow of goods and services. Many of these agreements were later extended to neighboring Kyrgyzstan, establishing the Central Asian Union. In 1998 Tajikistan also joined this regional alliance.

A large number of ethnic Uzbeks live in neighboring countries. Up to 25 percent of the people residing in Tajikistan are of Uzbek descent, and Uzbeks account for roughly half a million people in each of the other Central Asian countries. Many Uzbeks fled to Afghanistan during Soviet rule. Today, they and their descendants may number as many as 2 million. With so many Uzbeks in other countries, the government of Uzbekistan has sometimes hinted that it must take on a broader role in the region. Understandably, such suggestions make Uzbekistan's Central Asian neighbors a bit nervous. They worry that Tashkent has dreams of regional hegemony (dominance).

Uzbekistan has developed the largest military in Central Asia—bigger, in fact, than the militaries of the other four countries combined. In the 1990s Uzbekistan dispatched troops to Tajikistan in support of that country's government, which was fighting a civil war with opposition groups. Yet concerns over cross-border terrorism led Uzbekistan to place land mines along its borders with Tajikistan and Kyrgyzstan in the Fergana Valley, which caused civilian casualties and strained relations.

Islam Karimov (right) poses with the presidents of (from left) Kyrgyzstan (Askar Akayev), Kazakhstan (Nursultan Nazarbayev), Tajikistan (Emomali Rakhmonov), and Russia (Vladimir Putin) at a meeting of the Central Asian Cooperation Organization. Uzbekistan's relations with its Central Asian neighbors and with Russia have seen a fair measure of friction, but the countries have also recognized the benefits of working together on various regional issues.

In May 2004 Kazakhstan signaled its interest in establishing a rail route from Druzhba, located on its border with China, to Iran and Turkey. Such a line would pass through Uzbekistan, which would require Kazakhstan and Uzbekistan to maintain good relations for construction and operation to take place.

Sometimes ecological problems can also foster international cooperation. The Central Asian countries have agreed to work together to solve the problem of the Aral Sea, and each has pledged money for this effort.

Russia and China

Uzbekistan's proximity to Russia and China—two nuclear-armed neighbors on the north and east—is, no doubt, a source of some apprehension for the small country's leaders. It is also strong motivation for Uzbekistan to cooperate in many areas, including economic development. Uzbekistan concluded formal treaties of trade and friendship with both Russia and China in the first decade of its existence as an independent state. In addition, Uzbekistan, Russia, and China are all members of the Shanghai Cooperation Organization, which was established in June 2001. This important regional alliance also includes Tajikistan, Kyrgyzstan, and Kazakhstan.

In many respects Uzbekistan's leaders may regard China as a more reliable partner than Russia—and as a better model for governance and economic development. It is not simply that Russian domination is a recent memory, or that Russia's economy has foundered while China's has boomed. China's Communist leadership, like the regime of Islam Karimov, seeks economic reform but appears to have no intention of relinquishing political control. Nevertheless, Uzbekistan's leaders seem determined not to permit Beijing's influence in the region to lead to Chinese hegemony in Central Asia. ("When the Chinese are in Central Asia," a regional proverb warns, "catastrophe follows.") Uzbekistan's leaders thus view good relations with the United States as an essential counterweight to Chinese (and, for that matter, Russian) influence.

China's relations with Uzbekistan and the other Central Asian countries are to a certain extent driven by a domestic consideration: in its northwestern Xinjiang region China has a restive population of Uygurs, a Turkic people also scattered throughout Central Asia. The Beijing government is intensely interested in stifling separatist movements among its Uygur population, and by offering friendly trade and diplomatic relations to the Central Asian countries, China provides an incentive for those countries to restrain their Uygur minorities. Indeed, China has attempted to frame Uygur nationalism in Xinjiang as part of the issue of international Islamic terrorism. Uzbekistan's Uygurs constitute a very small minority and have thus far remained at the political margins. But China has become an important trade partner for Uzbekistan, and a 2004 state visit to Tashkent by President Hu Jintao underscored Beijing's intention to maintain close links between the two countries.

The Middle East

Iran, Turkey, and the Arab countries all have ancient ties to Uzbekistan. Turkey was the first country to recognize Uzbekistan's independence and open an embassy in Tashkent. Almost immediately, Turkey began providing student scholarships and initiating economic agreements. The two countries have cooperated to fight drug trafficking.

Uzbekistan has signed trade agreements with both Jordan and Saudi Arabia, and Saudi Arabia has been active in financing the construction of mosques in Uzbekistan. Although Uzbekistan has supported the United States in its opposition to Iran, it also has pursued economic ventures with the Tehran government. Uzbekistan and Pakistan have coordinated to share gas pipelines and hydroelectric power. The Economic Cooperation Organization (ECO), whose original members were Pakistan, Iran, and Turkey, welcomed Uzbekistan, along with the four other Central Asian republics, Afghanistan, and Azerbaijan as new members in 1992.

While Uzbekistan has enjoyed friendly relations with Middle Eastern countries, developing economic ties with Israel—the longtime enemy of the Arab states—threaten to disrupt those relations. Uzbekistan and Israel have signed economic agreements regarding development, aviation links, and tourism, and Israel has provided aid to Uzbekistan for health care.

Karimov poses with Mohammad Khatami of Iran (center) and Hamid Karzai of Afghanistan in June 2003, after the three leaders had signed an agreement to build roads from the Central Asian nations to Iran.

The United States

Since 1993 the United States has maintained an embassy in Tashkent. That same year, the U.S. government began delivering humanitarian and technical aid to Uzbekistan, also granting the country Most-Favored-Nation trade status (now known as Normal Trade Relations). The amount of U.S. foreign aid to Uzbekistan has fluctuated through the years; aid has periodically been suspended in response to the Karimov government's failure to make progress in the areas of human rights and democratic reforms. Overall, however, American aid to Uzbekistan has grown tremendously since the United States launched its "war on terrorism" following the September 11, 2001, attacks on New York and Washington, D.C. In 2002 the United States gave Uzbekistan more than $160 million in aid.

That large aid package followed a watershed in U.S.-Uzbekistan relations: the signing, on March 12, of a strategic partnership agreement. In the agreement, the United States promised to reequip Uzbekistan's military forces. More important for policymakers in Tashkent, the pact contained what amounted to a U.S. security guarantee: the United States, it said, "would regard with grave concern any external threat" to Uzbekistan's security. Although the language was somewhat vague, Uzbekistan's leaders regarded this as a bulwark against possible threats from China or Russia.

U.S. financial aid and military and security commitments underscore Uzbekistan's continuing strategic importance to the United States. The air base at Karshi-Khanabad, home to some 1,000 American military personnel, was set up ahead of the U.S. invasion of Afghanistan, largely to provide a search-and-rescue capability. Subsequently, the base has been used for humanitarian missions. NATO has also expressed an interest in using Uzbekistan as a base for peacekeeping efforts in Afghanistan. With U.S. commitments in Afghanistan and Iraq, and with Iran a source of continuing concern to American policymakers, Uzbekistan will likely figure prominently in Washington's strategic planning for decades to come.

For its part, Uzbekistan has been a consistent supporter of the American war on terrorism, including the invasions of Afghanistan and Iraq. It stood alone as the sole Central Asian country to support the U.S.-led embargoes of both Iran and Iraq in the mid-1990s, and it has been a supporter of many other U.S. policies, including issues regarding Cuba.

Yet Uzbekistan's spotty record on human rights is a source of considerable discomfort in Washington. International organizations have made numerous demands that the United States monitor Uzbekistan's human rights policies and impose sanctions in the face of abuses. Such concerns impelled the U.S. government, in July 2004, to withhold an additional $18 million in aid that Uzbekistan would have been eligible to receive. But soon thereafter, the U.S. Department of Defense delivered $21 million in military assistance to Uzbekistan. This led many observers to conclude that, human rights issues notwithstanding, Washington remained committed to supporting Uzbekistan, the only Central Asian state with which it had a strategic partnership agreement.

Uzbekistan's minister of defense, Kodir Ghulomov (second from right, far side), hosts a meeting in Tashkent with U.S. military leaders, November 2001. Uzbekistan, a supportive partner in the U.S. "war on terrorism," will likely continue to figure prominently in U.S. strategic planning.

Europe

In 2002 the European Union–Uzbekistan Cooperation Council examined issues of justice and other local affairs. Generally, European Union (EU) countries have the same basic concerns regarding Uzbekistan as does the United States. The EU would like to see a firmer commitment to human rights and an expansion of democratic and economic reforms. At a meeting of the European Union–Uzbekistan Cooperation Council, Uzbekistan agreed to allow representatives of the International Red Cross to visit prisons and attend trials. In committing to this, government leaders in Uzbekistan hoped to put the EU's concerns to rest. In return, the European Union has pledged its assistance to improve the management of Uzbekistan's borders. Its primary goals are to stop drug traffickers and to assist refugees who are seeking asylum.

The Future

Uzbekistan's future remains uncertain. The government has exhibited an eagerness to develop international partnerships and economic cooperation with many nations, but greater democratic and economic reforms are necessary to achieve prosperity and long-term stability. Will Uzbekistan make the kinds of changes that are needed to advance its economic and political security in the 21st century? Will it be affected by the region's growing radical Islamic movements?

Hundreds of millions of dollars in U.S. aid will likely flow to Uzbekistan in the next few years, offering the country a unique opportunity to improve its economy and security. Whether gains in those areas will lead eventually to political reforms is by no means certain. The government has, in recent years, made several public displays of concern for human rights. In 2003, for example, 75 policemen accused of abusing, torturing, or killing prisoners were brought to trial; the following year, the government agreed to allow three international experts to observe the autopsy of a young man who had died in prison and whose family had accused prison officials of torture. But, critics say, such proceedings amount to mere window dressing; what is needed, they say, are sweeping and lasting reforms.

The literal translations of the words *uz* and *bek* are, respectively, "self" and "strong"—accurate words to describe the Uzbeks. Though remote during Soviet rule, Uzbekistan has been important to the world from the days of the Silk Road trade to the present. Over the centuries, the land and its inhabitants have endured invasions by some of history's most formidable conquerors. Finally, in the 21st century, the proud and resilient people of Uzbekistan have an opportunity to become masters of their own fate.

Fifth century B.C.:	The Bactrian, Soghdian, and Tokharian states dominate the area today known as Uzbekistan.
330 B.C.:	Alexander the Great begins conquering the region.
First century B.C.:	The trade route that becomes known as the Silk Road, which connects western Europe to the Far East, takes form in the Uzbekistan area and surrounding regions.
A.D. **710**:	Arabs conquer the region and successfully spread Islam.
819:	The Samanids become the first indigenous rulers since the Arab conquest; the dynasty rules for the rest of the century.
Early 11th century:	The Samanids conquer Khwarazm, a region encompassing land north and south of the Amu Dar'ya.
ca. 1200:	Genghis Khan and his Mongolian army invade Central Asia.
ca. 1380:	Timur successfully conquers the region and makes Samarqand his capital.
ca. 1500:	Shaybani Khan and the Uzbeks move into Uzbekistan.
ca. 1700:	Uzbekistan is divided into the three powerful khanates of Bukhara, Khiva, and Kokand.
1867–73:	Russia seizes the area of Karakalpak and goes on to conquer Bukhara, Kokand, and Khiva.
1917–18:	The Russian Revolution begins, followed by the formation of the Turkestan Autonomous Soviet Socialist Republic, which includes much of Uzbekistan; bitter fighting between Soviet forces and Uzbekistani nationalists in the Fergana Valley claims thousands of lives.

Chronology

1920: Russia establishes the People's Republic of Bukhara and the People's Republic of Khwarazm.

1924: The USSR's Central Committee establishes the Uzbek Soviet Socialist Republic (UzSSR).

1929: The Tajik Soviet Socialist Republic is separated from Uzbekistan.

1936: Karakalpakstan, an autonomous Soviet socialist republic, is joined with Uzbekistan.

1944: Soviet dictator Joseph Stalin orders the deportation of approximately 200,000 ethnic Tatars from the Crimea to Uzbekistan.

1959: Sharaf Rashidov becomes the first secretary of the Uzbekistan Communist Party.

1983: Rashidov is implicated in widespread corruption and fraud in Uzbekistan's cotton industry; the Soviet leadership begins purging the ranks of the Uzbek Communist Party.

1985: Mikhail Gorbachev gains power in the Soviet Union and initiates his policies of perestroika and glasnost, which eventually encourages public expression of discontent in Uzbekistan.

1989: Approximately 100 people die and more than 1,000 are injured in ethnic riots in the Fergana Valley; Islam Karimov becomes first secretary of the Uzbek Communist Party.

1990: Islam Karimov becomes executive president of the republic; the Communist Party of Uzbekistan declares sovereignty; Uzbek becomes the state language; following demonstrations, Tajiks living in Bukhara and Samarqand are given permission to use their own language.

1991: Following an abortive coup against Soviet leader Mikhail Gorbachev, the UzSSR declares independence and becomes the Republic of Uzbekistan; Karimov is reelected president; Uzbekistan is admitted to the CIS (Commonwealth of Independent States), the loose federation of republics that replaces the Soviet Union.

1992: A new constitution is adopted, granting more power to the president.

1993: Uzbekistan introduces its own currency, gains admission to the United Nations.

1997: A state of emergency is declared in Namangan and Andizhan in the Fergana Valley after militants kill an Uzbek police officer; several mosques are closed and about 1,000 people are arrested.

1998: After Taliban forces seize territory in northern Afghanistan, the government of Uzbekistan begins a campaign aimed at eradicating radical Islam.

1999: A half-dozen bombs in Tashkent kill 16 and injure more than 150, prompting a renewed crackdown against Islamic extremists and other opposition groups.

2002: A constitutional amendment is passed to extend the president's term from five to seven years; Uzbekistan and the United States sign a strategic partnership agreement on March 12.

2003: A decree is issued requiring all foreign nongovernmental organizations (NGOs) to reregister with the Uzbekistan Justice Ministry; in a speech before the North Atlantic Treaty

Organization (NATO), Vladimir Norov, Uzbekistan's deputy minister of foreign affairs, confirms Uzbekistan's commitment to reconstruction efforts in postwar Afghanistan.

2004: The Open Society Institute is told that it must leave Uzbekistan; three U.S.-funded NGOs receive warnings against collaborating with unregistered agencies; more than 40 people die in four days of bomb attacks in March; in July, suicide bombers strike Uzbekistan's prosecutor general's office and also target the U.S. and Israeli embassies; in December, elections are held for Uzbekistan's parliament, the Oliy Majlis (including the new lower house).

arable—capable of being used for the growing of crops.

authoritarian—relating to a system of government in which one leader has total control and is not responsible to the people.

autonomous—existing independently; having the right of self-government.

city-state—an independent, autonomous city and the surrounding territory that it controls.

caliphate—an Islamic political dominion under the rule of a caliph (a Muslim spiritual and temporal leader) and following *Sharia* (Islamic law).

coup—the sudden overthrow of a government (usually by the military), using force or the threat of force.

Cyrillic—relating to an alphabet used for writing Russian or other languages of eastern Europe and Asia.

delta—the deposit of clay, silt, sand, and other materials at the mouth of a river.

desertification—the process by which arable land is converted to desert, often through poor agricultural practices.

enclaves—territories or culturally distinct groups situated within a foreign country.

flyway—a route used seasonally by migrating birds.

glasnost—a policy begun by Mikhail Gorbachev to make the government of the Soviet Union less secretive and more open to citizens.

indigenous—born and living in a specific region.

iron curtain—a term used to describe the ideological, political, and military barrier that isolated the Soviet Union and Eastern Europe from the rest of the world.

khanate—the territory ruled by a khan.

market economy—an economy that operates by voluntary exchange and is not controlled by a central authority.

metallurgy—the science and technology of metals, especially extracting metals from ore.

Glossary

nomadic—traveling from place to place rather than having a fixed home.

perestroika—a policy begun by Mikhail Gorbachev to restructure the government and economy of the Soviet Union.

political dissidents—people who take a stand in opposition to their government.

political purges—attempts to remove anyone thought to be disloyal to the government.

polytheistic—worshiping more than one god.

secular—not religious.

sovereignty—independence; freedom from external control.

steppe—a large area of treeless, usually level, and dry grassland.

subsidy—monetary assistance from the government that often supports needed products or services.

underemployment—a situation in which workers, though employed, work only part time, for minimal compensation, or in positions that are below their skill level.

Alaolmolki, Nozar. *Life After the Soviet Union*. Albany: State University of New York, 2001.

Critchlow, James. *Nationalism in Uzbekistan: A Soviet Republic's Road to Sovereignty*. Boulder, Colo.: Westview Press, 1991.

Hunter, Shireen T. *Islam in Russia: The Politics of Identity and Security*. Armonk, N.Y.: M.E. Sharpe, 2004.

Kleveman, Lutz. *The New Great Game: Blood and Oil in Central Asia*. New York: Atlantic Monthly Press, 2003.

Melvin, Neil J. *Uzbekistan: Transition to Authoritarianism on the Silk Road*. Newark, N.J.: Harwood Academic Publishers, 2000.

Rashid, Ahmed. *Jihad: The Rise of Militant Islam in Central Asia*. New York: Penguin Books, 2002.

Sengupta, Anita. *The Formation of the Uzbek Nation-State: A Study in Transition*. Oxford, U.K.: Lexington Books, 2004.

Soucek, Svat. *A History of Inner Asia*. Cambridge, U.K.: University of Cambridge Press, 2000.

Thubron, Colin. *The Lost Heart of Asia*. New York: HarperCollins Publishers, 1994.

Visson, Lynn. *The Art of Uzbek Cooking*. New York: Hippocrene Books, 1998.

Internet Resources

http://www.cia.gov/cia/publications/factbook/geos/uz.html

The CIA World Factbook provides useful general information about Uzbekistan.

http://www.hrw.org/reports/2003/uzbekistan0903/7.htm

Learn about human rights issues in Uzbekistan from this Web page from Human Rights Watch.

http://www.uzbekconsulny.org/uzbekistan/socialprofile/

The official site of the Consulate General of Uzbekistan in New York City provides an overview of Uzbek culture and a number of useful links to sites devoted to the country.

http://www.uzland.uz/english/

This page contains a number of in-depth articles on the important issues that Uzbekistan faces.

http://www.fpri.org/enotes/20040412.americawar.seiple. terroruzbekistan.html

This essay by Chris Seiple, president of the Institute for Global Engagement, explores the significance of the 2004 terrorist attacks in Uzbekistan.

Numbers in **bold italic** refer to captions.

Index

Index

Picture Credits

The **FOREIGN POLICY RESEARCH INSTITUTE (FPRI)** served as editorial consultants for the GROWTH AND INFLUENCE OF ISLAM IN THE NATIONS OF ASIA AND CENTRAL ASIA series. FPRI is one of the nation's oldest "think tanks." The Institute's Middle East Program focuses on Gulf security, monitors the Arab-Israeli peace process, and sponsors an annual conference for teachers on the Middle East, plus periodic briefings on key developments in the region.

Among the FPRI's trustees is a former Secretary of State and a former Secretary of the Navy (and among the FPRI's former trustees and interns, two current Undersecretaries of Defense), not to mention two university presidents emeritus, a foundation president, and several active or retired corporate CEOs.

The scholars of FPRI include a former aide to three U.S. Secretaries of State, a Pulitzer Prize–winning historian, a former president of Swarthmore College and a Bancroft Prize–winning historian, and two former staff members of the National Security Council. And the FPRI counts among its extended network of scholars—especially its Inter-University Study Groups—representatives of diverse disciplines, including political science, history, economics, law, management, religion, sociology, and psychology.

DR. HARVEY SICHERMAN is president and director of the Foreign Policy Research Institute in Philadelphia. He has extensive experience in writing, research, and analysis of U.S. foreign and national security policy, both in government and out. He served as Special Assistant to Secretary of State Alexander M. Haig Jr. and as a member of the Policy Planning Staff of Secretary of State James A. Baker III. Dr. Sicherman was also a consultant to Secretary of the Navy John F. Lehman Jr. (1982–1987) and Secretary of State George Shultz (1988).

A graduate of the University of Scranton (B.S., History, 1966), Dr. Sicherman earned his Ph.D. at the University of Pennsylvania (Political Science, 1971), where he received a Salvatori Fellowship. He is author or editor of numerous books and articles, including *America the Vulnerable: Our Military Problems and How to Fix Them* (FPRI, 2002) and *Palestinian Autonomy, Self-Government and Peace* (Westview Press, 1993). He edits *Peacefacts*, an FPRI bulletin that monitors the Arab-Israeli peace process.

JOYCE LIBAL is a graduate of the University of Wisconsin–Green Bay. Before becoming a magazine editor and a writer, she was one of the founding board members of ECOLOGIA (www.ecologia.org), a nonprofit organization formed to assist environmentalists in the former Soviet Union. Joyce spent five years working as Program Director of ECOLOGIA, during which she traveled to several former Soviet republics and worked as a curriculum developer on a project that produced an environmental curriculum for schoolchildren in 17 countries. Today, she is an editor and writer living in northeastern Pennsylvania.